INSTRUCTOR'S MANUAL AND TEST BANK FOR

DUFFY • WONG
COMMUNITY PSYCHOLOGY

Myles S. Faith
Hofstra University

Kenneth M. Carpenter
Hofstra University

Allyn and Bacon
Boston · London · Toronto · Sydney · Tokyo · Singapore

Copyright © 1996 by Allyn & Bacon
A Simon & Schuster Company
Needham Heights, Massachusetts 02194

All rights reserved. The contents, or parts thereof, may be reproduced for use with *Community Psychology,* by Karen Grover Duffy and Frank Y. Wong, provided such reproductions bear copyright notice, but may not be reproduced in any form for any other purpose without written permission from the copyright owner.

ISBN 0-205-17448-5

Printed in the United States of America

10 9 8 7 6 5 4 3 2 1   00 99 98 97 96 95

CONTENTS

	Page
PREFACE	1
CHAPTER 1: INTRODUCTION TO COMMUNITY PSYCHOLOGY	2
Lectures and Notes	2
Multiple Choice Questions	4
Identification of Terms	10
Food For Thought	11
Key Terms	12
Recommended Films	12
CHAPTER 2: SCIENTIFIC RESEARCH METHODS	14
Lectures and Notes	14
Multiple Choice Questions	21
Identification of Terms	28
Food For Thought	28
Key Terms	31
Recommended Films	32
CHAPTER 3: THE IMPORTANCE OF SOCIAL CHANGE	33
Lectures and Notes	33
Multiple Choice Questions	37
Identification of Terms	42
Food For Thought	43
Key Terms	44
Recommended Films	44
CHAPTER 4: CREATING AND SUSTAINING SOCIAL CHANGE	45
Lectures and Notes	45
Multiple Choice Questions	49
Identification of Terms	55
Food For Thought	55
Key Terms	56
Recommended Films	56
CHAPTER 5: STRESS, COPING, AND SOCIAL SUPPORT: TOWARD COMMUNITY MENTAL HEALTH	58
Lectures and Notes	58
Multiple Choice Questions	62
Identification of Terms	68
Food For Thought	69
Key Terms	69
Recommended Films	71
CHAPTER 6: THE SERIOUS MENTALLY DISORDERED: BACK TO THE THE COMMUNITY	72
Lectures and Notes	72
Multiple Choice Questions	77
Identification of Terms	85
Food For Thought	85
Key Terms	86
Recommended Films	87

CHAPTER 7: SOCIAL AND HUMAN SERVICES IN THE COMMUNITY...... 89
    Lectures and Notes.................................. 89
    Multiple Choice Questions........................... 94
    Identification of Terms.............................101
    Food For Thought....................................102
    Key Terms...103
    Recommended Films...................................103

CHAPTER 8: SCHOOLS, CHILDREN, AND COMMUNITY.................105
    Lectures and Notes..................................105
    Multiple Choice Questions...........................110
    Identification of Terms.............................119
    Food For Thought....................................119
    Key Terms...120
    Recommended Films...................................120

CHAPTER 9: LAW, CRIME, AND THE COMMUNITY....................123
    Lectures and Notes..................................123
    Multiple Choice Questions...........................129
    Identification of Terms.............................135
    Food For Thought....................................136
    Key Terms...137
    Recommended Films...................................137

CHAPTER 10: THE HEALTH CARE SYSTEM..........................139
    Lectures and Notes..................................139
    Multiple Choice Questions...........................142
    Identification of Terms.............................147
    Food For Thought....................................148
    Key Terms...148
    Recommended Films...................................149

CHAPTER 11: COMMUNITY ORGANIZATIONAL PSYCHOLOGY.............151
    Lectures and Notes..................................151
    Multiple Choice Questions...........................157
    Identification of Terms.............................164
    Food For Thought....................................165
    Key Terms...165
    Recommended Films...................................166

CHAPTER 12: THE FUTURE OF COMMUNITY PSYCHOLOGY..............168
    Lectures and Notes..................................168
    Multiple Choice Questions...........................170
    Identification of Terms.............................174
    Food For Thought....................................175
    Key Terms...176
    Recommended Films...................................176

PREFACE

This Instructor's Manual is designed to accompany *Community Psychology* by K. Duffy and F.Y. Wong. It is the authors' goal to provide instructors with a manual that highlights the important concepts and facts presented to students of community psychology. Furthermore, each chapter contains test questions, identification of terms, open ended questions, and suggested films designed to augment the lecture material provided to the instructor. All chapters are divided into six sections. They include:

1. Lectures and Notes: designed to outline each chapter's major sections and provide the instructor with an outline of all important points presented to the students in their reading.

2. Multiple Choice Questions: provide the instructor with approximately 50 to 60 multiple choice questions relating to the material covered within each chapter. Answers for all questions are indicated by an "*" next to the correct response.

3. Identification of Terms: Designed to provide the instructor with definitional questions related to key terms highlighted in each chapter.

4. Food for Thought: Contains approximately four to five essay type questions designed to assess the student's ability to incorporate and apply the various factual and conceptual points presented in each chapter. The instructor is provided with answer notes highlighting some of the important points which should be included in the student's answer.

5. Key Terms: Every chapter includes a list of the highlighted terms presented in the text. Some of these terms are presented in the identification of terms section.

6. Recommended Films: Designed to provide the instructor with auxiliary resources which correspond with the material covered in each chapter.

To conserve space, the references cited in this manual can be found in the Reference section of Duffy and Wong's text book. The authors of this manual would like to thank both Drs. F.Y. Wong and K. Duffy for their support during the preparation of this manual.

CHAPTER 1

INTRODUCTION TO COMMUNITY PSYCHOLOGY

Introduction

This chapter introduces students to the field of community psychology by presenting an historical overview of the field. One important theme was the growing dissatisfaction among health care providers which eventually fueled the growth of community psychology. Specifically, clinicians felt the need to change more than the individual. Rather, social change was deemed necessary to reach greater numbers of people.

The chapter then discusses the philosophy and goals of community psychology, which emphasize prevention, the empowerment of individuals, and the development of a sense of community. The chapter ends by reviewing educational and work opportunities within the field.

Lectures and Notes

I. Historical Background

Social problems have always existed. However, formal social programs and psychological interventions have not always been needed to address them. For example, in the colonial United States, close-knit, agrarian communities typically cared for individual persons. However, with increased industrialization and the expanded size of cities, communities could no longer easily contain social problems. Institutionalization became the standard "intervention" for the mentally ill, indigent, and other powerless persons. These individuals were typically exposed to inhumane living conditions and treated by restraint as well as other forms of punishment. Immigrants entering the United States in the 1700's were frequently diagnosed as being mentally deficient and filtered to overpopulated institutions.

With the advent of psychoanalysis in the 1800's, Sigmund Freud attempted to treat psychopathology at the level of the individual. For example, by uncovering an alcoholic mother's unconscious and destructive drives, excessive drinking is best understood and treated. Freud emphasized individual weakness rather than strength. Towards the end of Freud's death, however, World War II began and the demand for professional psychologists to treat soldiers increased.

In the middle of the twentieth century, the Federal Government became more actively involved in addressing social problems. The National Mental Health Act was passed in 1946. Shortly thereafter, the National Institute for Mental Health was established. In 1949, the United States Public Health Service sponsored a conference in Boulder, Colorado. This famous conference introduced a training model for clinical psychologists which emphasized an integration of science and practice.

In the 1950's, new psychoactive drugs (antipsychotics, tranquilizers, and antidepressants) were increasingly dispensed within hospitals to treat various disorders. Concurrently, the field of clinical psychology and psychiatry was under considerable scrutiny. Seminal publications by Szasz (1961), Eysenck (1954, 1960), and Meehl (1954) challenged the efficacy of psychotherapy and the "myth" of mental illness.

Did controversies from the 1950's impede the evolution of community psychology? No. The Civil Rights Movement forged into the 1960's, fighting for the rights of minorities, women, and other underprivileged. President John Kennedy helped to pass the Community Mental Health Centers Act of 1963 which authorized funds for local mental health services. Particularly noteworthy was the conference held in Swampscott, Massachusetts, which is cited as the official birth date of community psychology. At this conference, clinical psychologists expressed their dissatisfaction with individual client changes and called for greater political activism. Other influential conferences followed. These efforts led to the establishment of Division 27 (Community Psychology) within the American Psychological Association, as well as the establishment of peer-review journals (e.g., Journal of Community Psychology, American Journal of Community Psychology, Journal of Rural Community Psychology).

II. Philosophy and Goals of Community Psychology

Before defining a field's philosophy and goals, it is essential to define that field. Specifically, "community psychology focuses on social issues, social institutions, and other settings which influence individuals, groups, and organizations. The goal is to optimize the well-being of individuals and communities with innovative and alternative interventions designed in collaboration with affected community members and with other related disciplines inside and outside of psychology."

Community psychology emphasizes...

* Prevention rather than treatment. Primary prevention attempts to prevent a problem from occurring altogether. Secondary prevention attempts to contain and treat a problem before reaching severe levels. Tertiary treatment attempts to treat already severe and pervasive problems.

* Strengths rather than weaknesses. Unlike Freud's emphasis on personal weakness, community psychologists focus on competency and mastery (White, 1959).

* Ecological Perspective. Environments influence people and people influence their environments. Along these lines, the ecological perspective searches for the optimal person-environment fit. That is, how can the person-environment relationship be arranged so as to reduce human suffering and maximize human potential?

* Respect for Diversity. Although only 11% of the articles in community psychology journals pertain to ethnic minorities, community psychology continues to strive toward ethnic, racial, and sexual diversity.

* Empowerment. Individuals can learn to increase control over their environments.

* Choice and Accessibility to social services.

* Action Research. Theory needs to move from the clouds down to Earth! That is, theoretically driven research should be used for resolving

social problems.

* Social Change

* Interdisciplinary Collaboration. Even the best psychologists benefit from alternative perspectives (e.g., economics, history, biology, sociology, and anthropology).

* Sense of Community. A strong sense of community is associated with increased voting, working on public policy, and contacting public officials. Also, neighborhood satisfaction is common to city dwellers as well as suburbanites. A sense of community is comprised of (a) membership (b) influence (c) integration and (d) a sense of emotional connection.

III. Community Psychology Today

Paul Speer and colleagues (1992) have studied trends within the field during the past decade. They have done so by tracking publications within two of the leading community psychology journals between 1984 and 1988. Their review indicated that the number of experimental studies decreased during this period, while the number of field studies increased. Similarly, fewer studies have used control groups in recent years. Also, participants identified with psychological problems were less likely to appear in recent than older studies. According to Speer et al., these findings suggest (a) a greater preference for qualitative research in recent years, and (b) a preference for studying larger community sectors where problems occur.

IV. Community Psychology Today--What's In It For You

A greater appreciation for community psychology is obtained from undergraduate classes, community volunteer programs, or graduate (Masters/Ph. D.) programs. Research by Snyder and Omoto (1982) found that over 80% of the AIDS volunteers whom they interviewed got involved due to self-initiation. People who quit volunteer work typically did so because of time constraints and stigmatization. People who stayed in the program reported greater levels of self-satisfaction, learning, and skills acquisitions compared to quitters.

Graduates of advanced programs also appear to be satisfied with their careers. One study reported a 90% employment rate among graduates, with 75% working in human services and 94% reporting moderate to high job satisfaction (Hoffnung, Morris, & Jex, 1986). Another study found that 83% of the graduates obtained their first choice agency job (Walfish, Polifka, & Stenmark, 1986). Several countries, including Israel, have schools which train community activists.

Multiple Choice Questions

1) The colonial United States was characterized by
   a. expanding industrialization.
   b. institutionalization of immigrants.
 * c. cohesive communities oriented towards the individual.
   d. growing dissatisfaction among clinical psychologists.

2) Sigmund Freud's psychoanalysis emphasized _____ rather than _____.
   a. strength; weakness
   b. community; the individual
 * c. the unconscious; the conscious
   d. none of the above is correct.

3) President John Kennedy was influential in securing ...
   a. the Boulder Conference.
 * b. the Community Mental Health Centers Act of 1963.
   c. the Swampscott Conference.
   d. the National Mental Health Act.

4) Hans Eysenck Sr. argued that ...
   a. mental illness was a "myth."
 * b. psychotherapy was as often useful as the mere passage of time.
   c. psychoanalysis was effective for treating unconscious drives.
   d. none of the above is correct.

5) When your child gets an ear infection and is immediately taken to the doctor for a cure, this is an example of ...
   a. primary prevention.
 * b. secondary prevention.
   c. tertiary prevention.

6) Many sex educators argue that sex education should be taught in the schools as early as possible. This approach to AIDS reduction is an example of ...
 * a. primary prevention.
   b. secondary prevention.
   c. tertiary prevention.
   d. none of the above.

7) Community psychologists emphasize all of the following except
   a. competence.
   b. the importance of tertiary prevention.
   c. community choices.
   d. empowerment of minorities.
 * e. all of the above are emphasized by community psychologists.

8) According to research by Adams (1992), satisfaction with one's community ...
   a. is more common in inner-cities than in suburbs.
   b. is more common in suburbs than in inner-cities.
 * c. is about equally common in suburbs and inner-cities.
   d. is unrelated to citizen voting habits.

9) A sense of community consists of all of the following except
   a. membership.
   b. integration.
 * c. individualism.
   d. emotional connection.

10) Speer et al.'s (1992) review of the top two community psychology journals found which of the following trends between 1984 and 1988?
   a. fewer studies using participants identified with psychological problems.
   b. more studies using control groups.
   c. fewer field studies.
 * d. less reporting of participants' gender and ethnicity.

11) Based on their review of the published literature between 1984 and 1988, Speer et al. (1992) concluded that ...
   a. community psychologists' research has become less sophisticated over the years.
 * b. the field is paying more attention to problems as and where they occur.
   c. the field is moving away from the study of diverse populations.
   d. all of the above are true.

12) Snyder and Omoto (1982) studied the reasons that people volunteered to do AIDS work. They found that ...
 * a. most people volunteered because they wanted to do so.
   b. most people volunteered because they had to do so.
   c. volunteers did not feel stigmatized by their work.
   d. initial motivation had little relationship to the amount of time people stayed on as volunteers.

13) Hoffnung, Morris and Jex (1986) reported that graduates of masters programs in community psychology have an employment rate of ...
   a. 30%
   b. 50%
   c. 75%
 * d. 90%

14) York and Havassy (1993) described advocacy programs in ...
 * a. Israel
   b. Germany
   c. Canada
   d. Sweeden

15) When theory-based research strives toward the reduction of social problems, we call this ...
   a. empowerment
 * b. action research
   c. person-environment fit
   d. collaboration

16) In the past decade, research in community psychology has seen ...
   a. an increase in experiments
 * b. a decrease in the use of control groups
   c. a decrease in the number of field studies
   d. none of the above

17) Which of the following statements is true?
    a. Clinical psychologists have a medical degree
  * b. Clinical psychologists cannot prescribe medication
    c. Clinical psychology began to thrive as a field with the passage of the National Mental Health Act of 1946.
    d. All of the above are true

18) Look at the following list of historical events:
    (1) Pinel's attempt at institutional reforms
    (2) Swampscott Conference
    (3) Publications by Eysenck
    (4) World War II
    (5) Freud's classic works on Psychoanalysis

   Which of the following represents the correct order of these five historical events:

    a. 1,5,4,3,2
    b. 1,2,3,4,5
  * c. 5,1,4,3,2
    d. 5,3,1,4,2

19) Approximately _____ of articles comprising the community psychology literature is pertinent to ethnic minorities.
  * a. 10%
    b. 25%
    c. 50%
    d. 75%

20) According to research by Walfish, Polifka, and Stenmark (1986), graduates of community psychology programs...
    a. feel most competent in designing intervention programs.
    b. feel least competent in program evaluation and needs assessment.
    c. do not get jobs which are their "first choices."
  * d. feel they need more training in community empowerment processes.

21. Which of the following individuals or places is most strongly associated with the birth of community psychology?
    a. Sigmund Freud
    b. Robert White
    c. Community Mental Health Centers Act of 1963
  * d. Swampscott, MA

22. Robert White is noted for his writings on ...
  * a. competence
    b. psychoanalysis
    c. empowerment
    d. respect for diversity

23. John wants to become a community psychologist. Probably the best way for him to get thorough, comprehensive training would be to ...
    a. get real-world experience by doing volunteer work
    b. get a government job
  * c. get a Masters or Ph.D. in community psychology
    d. take advanced undergraduate classes

24. Which of the following professional is (are) trained and licensed to prescribe medication to clients?
    a. community psychologists
    b. clinical psychologists
  * c. psychiatrists
    d. both B and C

25. Psychology's recognition that life experiences play a crucial role in shaping mental health was greatly influenced by ...
    a. World War I
    b. World War II
    c. Psychoanalysis
  * d. All of the above

26. Klingman (1985) studied the prevention of children's anxiety about ...
  * a. rubella vaccinations
    b. chicken pox
    c. tetanus vaccinations
    d. suicide

27. Community psychologists are likely to work in which of the following settings?
    a. universities
    b. consulting firms
    c. medical schools
  * d. all of the above

28. With which statement(s) would the community psychologist agree?
    a. The role of the community psychologist is to promote the well-being and community life of the average citizen.
    b. Prevention before a problem develops is better than treatment after the fact.
    c. The bias in other areas of psychology is to be too "person-centered."
  * d. All of the above.

29. Which of the following is the best example of empowerment?
  * a. allowing a group of school children to decide where they want to go on a field trip.
    b. a judge ordering a criminal to go for a psychiatric examination.
    c. the college president asking for advice on the college calendar but perhaps not following that advice when given.
    d. none of the above

30. The ecological focus of community psychology emphasizes...
    a. the conversations between patient and therapist.
  * b. the interaction between the person and environment.
    c. the role of age and social class in the development of mental disorders.
    d. the diminished role of management in the modern organization.

31. Of the three major forces in psychology, which has had the most impact on community psychology?
    a. Freudianism or psychoanalysis
    b. behaviorism or Skinnerian psychology
  * c. Humanism or Rogerian/Maslowian psychology
    d. all three have had an equal impact

32. Eysenck's research (his literature review) of the psychotherapeutic literature shocked psychologists as he showed that ...
    a. therapy is too expensive
  * b. control groups often spontaneously become better as often as treatment groups
    c. half of all therapists had some sort of sexual encounter with their clients
    d. none of the above

33. With which statement would community psychologists agree the most?
    a. we should respect the diversity of people in communities.
    b. psychologists should take their services to the people rather than make people come to psychologists
    c. social innovation and reform are beneficial
  * d. all of these

34. Which of the following best summarizes the progress of community psychology journals in terms of their coverage of ethnic minorities?
    a. poor and getting worse
  * b. some progress, but much more needed
    c. very satisfactory at the moment
    d. good for Asian Americans; poor for Hispanic Americans

35. With which of the following statements would most community psychologists agree.
  * a. depressed individuals should have accessibility to all available treatment options and should be allowed to select their own treatment
    b. government should determine and legalize the "best" treatment options for depression. Then, depressed persons should be allowed to select which of these alternatives they want to peruse.
    c. wealthy individuals should have less accessibility to the best treatment services
    d. both A & C

36. The destruction of the Berlin Wall in Germany is an example of ...
    a. action research
  * b. unplanned social change
    c. competence
    d. planned social change

37. Individuals graduating with a Ph.D. in community psychology should expect...
    a. an atypically long period of unemployment
  * b. job satisfaction
    c. difficulties getting their first-choice job, especially if it is university position
    d. never to work in a medical school.

38. With its emphasis on prevention, community psychologists might be described as...
   a. reactive
   b. tertiary
 * c. proactive
   d. discouraging empowerment

39. Over the decade the number of _____ within community psychology journals have decreased while the number of _____ have increased.
 * a. experiments; field studies
   b. field studies; experiments
   c. field studies; studies using control groups
   d. experiments; studies using control groups

40. According to research by Walfish et al. (1984), graduates of community psychology would benefit from more training in...
   a. evaluation and needs assessment
 * b. intervention skills
   c. empowerment processes
   d. all of the above

Identification of Terms

1. Freud's treatment method for mental illness. (Answer=psychoanalysis).

2. Conference cited as birth site of community psychology. (Answer=Swampscott).

3. The process of enhancing the probability that people can control their own lives. (Answer=empowerment).

4. The utilization of theory-grounded research for the resolution of social problems. (Answer=action research).

5. Scientific study in which variables are manipulated. (Answer=experiment).

6. Field within psychology which deals with diagnosis, measurement, and treatment of mental illness. (Answer=clinical psychology).

7. Efforts to prevent a problems from occurring altogether. (Answer=primary prevention).

8. Efforts to treat a problem at the earliest possible moment before it becomes severe or persistent. (Answer=secondary prevention).

9. Efforts to reduce the severity of a problem once it has persistently occurred. (Answer=tertiary prevention).

10. Changes in the community which occur in a spontaneous, even revolutionary, manner (Answer=unplanned social change).

Food For Thought

1. Imagine that your younger brother, Steven, approaches you with a big smile on his face. He is happy because he just decided to become a clinical psychologist. He wants to open a private practice and treat individual clients with problems. Also, Steven heard that most community psychologists are unhappy with their career decisions. As a community psychologist yourself, what concerns do you have for your younger brother. In what ways will your brother be satisfied or dissatisfied with his outlook? Do you agree with your brother's beliefs? Why or why not? Justify your answers with historical evidence and empirical data.

[Answer Notes: Discuss clinical psychologists' dissatisfaction with their inability to facilitate social change. Also, discuss numerous studies indicating job satisfaction and employment among community psychologists]

II. Society has an increasing number of cocaine- and crack-addicted mothers. Imagine that you have just been promoted as the United States Surgeon General. How would you tackle this problem using (a) primary prevention, (b) secondary prevention, and (c) tertiary prevention? Describe three brief treatment programs--each one designed according to one of the three prevention strategies. How do your programs differ? How are they similar? What are their advantages and disadvantages? Which one do YOU personally like the best? Why?

[Answer Note: Answers should reflect an understanding for the fundamental differences between primary vs. secondary vs. tertiary prevention. Students should appreciate their distinct advantages of primary prevention]

III. Imagine that you just graduated with a Ph.D. in community psychology. What career path would you follow? What would be your ideal job? Which jobs wouldn't you want and why? What changes would you hope to make at your job?

[Answer Note: Answers should reflect an understanding for the diversity of job opportunities available to community psychologists. Students should focus which aspects of the field They prefer more than others.]

IV. Imagine that you are the keynote speaker at the Swampscott Conference. Write out a speech in which you present to your audience (clinical psychologists, community psychologists, and psychiatrists) the rationale for the current conference, its mission and goals, and your plans for a Swampscott reunion in the year 2000.

V. Describe the influence of Psychoanalysis and both World Wars in terms of how they helped to shape the community psychology. Why were they "necessary ingredients" for growing dissatisfaction in psychology and the call for change?

[Answer Note: Answers should focus on Freud's individualism and the greater attention paid to environmental contributions to mental illness].

Key Terms

Action research
Attribution theory
Clinical psychology
Community
Community psychology
Competence
Control groups
Ecological perspective
Empowerment
Experiments
Field studies
Fundamental attribution error
Neighboring
Person-environment fit
Planned social change
Prevention
Primary prevention
Psychiatry
Social support
Secondary prevention
Sense of community
Social psychology
Social support
Tertiary prevention
Prevention

Recommended Films

Black Power In America: Myth Or Reality? (59 minutes). Through candid interviews with Clifton Wharton, Eleanor Holmes Norton, Arthur Ashe, and Don King, this documentary surveys some of the changes in American society since the civil right's movement of the 1960's. Insight Media Inc., 2162 Broadway, New York, New York, 10024.

Chicanos In Transition (30 minutes). This documentary examines the lifestyles of the Chicanos living in a small community in Ohio, exploring how they maintain their tradition while assimilating aspects of Anglo culture. Insight Media Inc., 2162 Broadway, New York, New York, 10024.

Culture (30 minutes). Traveling to different regions of the United States, this program portrays cultural diversity, showing that different subcultures address human needs in different ways. Insight Media Inc., 2162 Broadway, New York, New York, 10024.

Introduction To Culture and Diversity (60 minutes). Defining the terms culture, macroculture, and microculture, this discussion considers the many cultures and religious groups in the United States. Insight Media Inc., 2162 Broadway, New York, New York, 10024.

Hispanic-American Cultures (60 minutes). Focusing on the ethnic groups classified as Hispanics, this program examines issues facing Hispanic communities in the United States and highlights the diversity of this group of people. Insight Media Inc., 2162 Broadway, New York, New York, 10024.

Is Cultural Diversity A Good Idea? (30 minutes). Discussing whether or not cultural diversity is a desirable goal, experts probe the role of African Americans and women in higher education. Insight Media Inc., 2162 Broadway, New York, New York, 10024.

The Rage for Democracy (60 minutes). Four stories test the ideal of democracy against the reality of everyday life, investigating the influence of race, income, and education on citizen activism. PBS Video Catalogue. 1320 Braddock Place, Alexandria, VA, 22314-1698.

Native-American Cultures (Part 2) (58 minutes). This program explores moral and ethical issues related to the rights of Native Americans. Insight Media Inc., 2162 Broadway, New York, New York, 10024.

Overcoming Prejudice In A Multicultural World (20 minutes). Illustrating the destructive nature of prejudice, this program teaches viewers to confront their own biases, as well as the biases of others. Insight Media Inc., 2162 Broadway, New York, New York, 10024.

Race, Hatred, and Violence: Searching For Solutions (22 minutes). Using interviews with community leaders, social activists, politicians, and legal and psychological experts, this program explores racism in American society, examining its causes and manifestations. Insight Media Inc., 2162 Broadway, New York, New York, 10024.

Racism (12 minutes). Filmed partly in South Central Los Angeles, this video talks to teenagers about hatred, unfair treatment, narrow mindedness, prejudice, stereotyping, and name calling. Insight Media Inc., 2162 Broadway, New York, New York, 10024.

Yo Soy (30 minutes). Probing concerns and problems of the Mexican-American community, this video examines the progress Chicanos have made in politics, education, and the labor force. PBS Video Catalogue. 1320 Braddock Place, Alexandria, VA, 22314-1698.

CHAPTER 2

SCIENTIFIC RESEARCH METHODS

Introduction

This chapter presents the philosophy of scientific research and a variety of research methodologies to students. First, students are taught the interaction between theory, design, and analysis, as well as the determinants of research fidelity. Systems theory is defined and emphasized to be an important concept for community psychologists. Students are then presented various research methodologies, both traditional and alternative, as well their respective strengths and weaknesses. Practical problems encountered by program evaluators working in real organizations are illustrated and solutions reviewed. Along these line, community psychologists must strive to fit within their environments and maintain cultural sensitivity.

Lectures and Notes

I. The Essence of Scientific Research

Why's and What's

Chapter 1 described community psychology as a field which attempts to orchestrate social change. The question then becomes how to evaluate whether or not these efforts are effective. That's where the "scientific method" (or, scientific research) comes into play. Scientific research provides community psychologists with a mechanism to evaluate the effectiveness of their interventions. Science forces us to bypass the simple "hunches" we all make when evaluating what goes on in the world. Although our "hunches" and "sixth senses" may be accurate, it is essential that psychologists have an armament of tools for rigorously testing them out. That's why scientific research is so important.

Several important concepts must be introduced in order to fully understand scientific research. One crucial concept is that of <u>theory</u>. A theory is a systematic attempt to explain observable events relating to an issue (e.g., alcoholism). By proposing relationships among variables, theories allow psychologists to make predictions about the world. The goal of a theory is to describe, predict, and control for <u>why</u> and <u>how</u> a variable (or variables) relate to real-world events. For example, one theory of alcoholism known as the "Tension Reduction" theory states that some individuals subjected to excessive amounts of stress will drink alcohol in order to reduce the stress. That is, this theory posits a relationship between two variables (i.e., stress and drinking).

A <u>model</u> is a working blueprint of a theory. It specifies which variables will be tested in an experiment. Some elaborate theories may have more than one model. A <u>paradigm</u> provides a smaller framework that guides researchers to conceptualize events in a consistent fashion.

The same behaviors can be described by different theories, as well as by different models. For example, the aforementioned tension reduction theory described drinking behavior in terms of perceived stress. A different theory of alcoholism argues that excessive drinking is the result of the inheritance of genetic predispositions. That is, alcoholism is due to one's genetic make-up. Thus, we now have a second theory of alcoholism. However, this one genetic theory may have two distinct models. One model may promote the investigation of the "guilty" genes; a second model may promote the investigation of alcohol consumption among identical versus fraternal twins. That is, the same theory can be tested through different models.

As Kuhn (1970) argued, theories do not change in a systematic fashion. Change is sporadic and often the result of a "crisis" within the field. For example, the field of community psychology was born out of a crisis within the field of psychology. That is, clinicians were dissatisfied with their ability to implement broad-based, social change.

One class of theory, systems theory, presumes that dynamic and fluctuating systems underlay psychological processes and human behavior. Systems are objects which relate to one another. More specifically, a system is an organized, unified network made up of interdependent components (or subsystems). System theories are particularly useful for community psychologists who try to understand dynamic relationships within and between groups.

Operational definitions provide specific, measurable indexes of concepts. For example, room temperature could be operationally defined with a Celsius thermometer. Alcohol consumption could be operationally defined by one's responses on an alcohol questionnaire.

An Independent Variable is a presumed cause of a dependent variable according to one's theoretical model. For example, according to D'Ercole at al.'s theory on alcohol and other drug use, coping skills, self-esteem, and pregnancy status determine amount of alcohol consumption. In this case, coping skills, self-esteem, and pregnancy status would all be independent variables. Alcohol consumption would be the dependent variable. Of course, all independent and dependent variables require specific operational definitions.

A design is a systematic plan to test out a hypothesis, including the measurement of the independent and dependent variables. As part of one's design, the researcher must decide upon his/her sampling strategy, that is, the process through which subjects will be recruited. Several common sampling strategies include:

* random sample--all individuals from the population of interest (e.g., alcoholics, pregnant women) have an equal opportunity to participate in the study. Unfortunately, true random sampling is often difficult to implement.

* convenience sample--individuals are selected for the study because they are easily available (e.g., college students in universities).

* purposive sample--specific individuals are targeted and chosen for a specific reason.

Once subjects are recruited, it is desirable to have random assignment of subjects to experimental conditions. For example, when testing the efficacy of a new medication, all subjects should ideally have the same odds of being assigned to a treatment or control condition. However, it is not always possible to randomly assign subjects to conditions. For example, federal guidelines mandate that no individuals should be denied access to the best possible treatment programs. Therefore, it may be unethical to assign some individuals to a control condition where they are denied a proven intervention.

Hypothesis testing is the process through which scientific activities are implemented. The essence of hypothesis testing, conceptualized by Popper's (1966) philosophy, is that scientific research cannot "prove" theories. This is impossible (after all, how could science UNEQUIVOCALLY and ABSOLUTELY be CERTAIN that stress causes drinking?). Rather, hypothesis testing is used to falsify and disprove the null hypothesis. The null hypothesis states that the results of one's research are simply due statistical chance or random error. For example, the null hypothesis states that any difference in drug use between pregnant women with good versus poor coping skills is solely due to random error or chance.

However, the goal of hypothesis testing is to do more than "reject the null." Rather, with the aid of a good theory, statistically significant findings are used to support an alternative hypothesis. For example, consistent with D'Ercole et al.'s theory, data might indicate that pregnant women with poor coping skills are more likely to use drugs than those with good coping skills. Such findings would mean a rejection of the null hypothesis (no true difference between groups) and support for the alternative hypothesis. Of course, the researcher's choice of statistical analysis will permit a quantitative mechanism for hypothesis testing.

Theory, design, and analysis are difficult to tease apart. They reciprocally determine one another. Theories are complex and only be tested fragment by fragment. However, theories are necessary for guiding one's research design and for providing alternative hypotheses when the null hypothesis is rejected.

The Fidelity of Research

Research fidelity refers to four related issues: ethics, reliability, internal validity, and external validity.

Ethics: Scientific research must protect the well-being of its participants, guarding them from physical, psychological, or social harm. Because of this, all researchers must first secure approval from an institutional review board before beginning their study.

Reliability: Reliability refers to the extent to which concrete or measurable features, or both, of a theory are replicable. For example, the tension reduction theory of alcohol would be reliable if numerous studies, using different research participants, consistently found greater incidence of drinking among individuals experiencing stress.

Internal Validity: Internal validity refers to the degree to which an independent variable is responsible for changes in a dependent variable. That is, it asks, "How much confidence does a researcher have that significant findings are really due to the manipulation of the independent variable(s)?" To the extent that there is high internal validity, confounding effects are minimized.

External Validity: External validity refers to the generalizability of results from a study to other studies or settings. For example, researchers in New York may find that women who enroll in a community-wide drug treatment program are less likely to use marijuana after one year. However, this intervention still needs to be evaluated in other locations.

As discussed in the chapter there are several important factors which influence research fidelity. These are selection bias, compensation, diffusion of treatment, experimental mortality, and maturational/historical events.

Selection Bias: Ideally, all potential participants for a study have the same chance of being selected for that study. Selection bias occurs to the extent that certain individuals are systematically excluded from participation. For example, all drug users should have an equal chance of being selected for an intervention designed for that population. However, if researchers only chose certain drug users (e.g., only those from low SES groups), they engage in selection bias.

Compensation: To the extent that research participants are not satisfied with their assignment within a study, they might compensate their responses and bias the results. For example, imagine that a woman wanting drug treatment were assigned to a no-treatment condition. Upset by this, the woman might indicate on drug use questionnaires that her drug use is worse than it actually is. This might be a ploy aimed at getting her into the drug treatment condition.

Diffusion of Treatment: Participants in studies often talk to one another and, consequently, bias one another's responses. This is called diffusion of treatment. For example, two women receiving alcohol counseling may converse about how effective services have been for them. The more they talk, the more strongly they believe that the intervention is effective. Such ardent beliefs may be artificially high and threaten the fidelity of the research.

Experimental Mortality: Participants often drop out of research studies. However, experimental mortality can be a problem if certain client characteristics (e.g., SES, age, education) are more strongly associated with attrition. Such findings would suggest systematic biases with an intervention.

Maturation/Historical Events: Maturation and historical events present threats to research fidelity if specific participant features (e.g., age, specific life experiences, cohort) interact with the effectiveness of the treatment intervention. For example, older individuals who remember alcohol prohibition in the United States may be more suspicious than younger individuals of abstinence-oriented treatment programs. That is, their life experience (having lived through prohibition) may interfere with their progress in a treatment program.

Community Researchers as Consultants

Research is often conducted by individuals called "consultants," who engage in collaborative problem-solving with one or more "consultees."

Consultees typically provide services to a third party called "clients." Given the collaborative nature of the consultation, consultees and clients are not referred to as subjects, but rather "participants."

Students should be aware that consultants work in a wide variety of settings, such as educational settings, industrial settings, governmental settings, and university public policy research laboratories. Despite this flexibility, consultants have often difficult jobs. For example, consultants might need to inform consultees (the same people who hired them) that they are part of the original problem! Furthermore, consultants must decide whether to use "outcome" or "process" measures when studying systems. Outcome measures assess the impact of an intervention (e.g., effects on self-esteem). Process measures assess transactions or processes which occur during an intervention (e.g., the implementation of programs designed to raise self-esteem).

Students should be aware that consultants do not simply try to "fix problems" for others. Rather, they try to empower the participants so that they can sustain any changes implemented by consultants. Along these lines, consultants need to take the perspective of the participants and elicit their support in problem-solving. This process is called "constituent validity." Of course, consultants must establish some mechanism to evaluate the effects of their interventions.

II. Traditional Scientific Research Methods

Students should be instructed that any research question can be studied with a variety of research methodologies. Several of the most common research methods are discussed by the authors, along with their respective strengths and limitations.

Correlational Method

The correlational method allows the researcher to determine the strength of association (or relationship) between two or more variables. For example, D'Ercole et al.'s theory predicts a relationship between pregnancy status (how many months a woman is pregnant) and the amount of alcohol she drinks. The "Pearson Correlation Coefficient" is the statistic used to measure the strength of association. This coefficient ranges from -1.00 to +1.00. The sign (- or +) determines the direction of the relationship, and the number (e.g., .79) indicates the magnitude. For example, a correlation of -.26 between months pregnant and alcohol consumption indicates that the longer a woman is pregnant, the less likely she is to drink alcohol. However, this relation appears to be a weak one.

The correlational method often relies upon good theory in order to make sense of significant association. This is because correlations do not indicate causation. For example, when interpreting the previous negative correlation, one cannot conclude that pregnancy causes less alcohol consumption. Why can't researchers infer causation from the correlational method? There is one main reason: CONTROL. Researchers using this method do not have control over what they are measuring. They only go out and examine the relationship between on-going life events. For example, researchers cannot control whether or not a woman becomes pregnant, nor whether or not she drinks. Also, because of this lack of control, spurious (false) correlations may emerge. For example, the correlation between pregnancy status and alcohol consumption may be a false one. That is, it may really be due to a third variable, for example, overall cardiovascular fitness. These relationships may go undetected in correlational research.

Experimental Method

The hallmark of the experimental method is CONTROL. Unlike with the correlational method, researchers using the experimental method control the independent and dependent variables. As a result, the researcher <u>can</u> make inferences about causality. The experimental includes a class of research designs and measurement techniques.

One common design is the <u>pretest-posttest control group design</u>. This design has two components. First, all participants are randomly assigned to either a treatment or control group. Second, all participants are measured at two points in time (typically before and after the treatment group has received its intervention). This design is particularly strong for evaluating the efficacy of new treatment programs.

Quasi-Experimental Methods

Unfortunately, many variables (e.g., pregnancy status) cannot be experimentally manipulated. A compromise is the quasi-experimental method, which allows the researcher some control over what he/she is studying.

A common design, the <u>nonequivalent pretest-posttest control design</u>, is identical to the pretest-posttest control group design with one exception. Specifically, participants are not randomly assigned to treatment and control groups. For example, a researcher may want to study differences in drug usage between pregnant and nonpregnant women at two points in time. Although this design is very practical, the experimenter cannot control for <u>all</u> differences between control and treatment participants. For example, pregnant and nonpregnant women differ in many ways (e.g., hormonally, socially, psychologically). It may be difficult to determine which drives group differences.

When research is conducted in natural world settings (e.g., the work office), it is referred to as field research. Field research uses both correlational and experimental methods.

III. Other Research Methods

As emphasized by the authors, research questions can be studied with diverse methodologies. Two alternative methodologies which have been frequently used by community psychologists include Ethnography and Epidemiology.

Ethnography refers to a broad class of research designs and measurement procedures/techniques which allow researchers to socially interact with participants. Unlike other methods, ethnography allows participants to describe their own experiences in their own words. Obviously, this method allows researchers to guide participants' verbal responses. For example, "participant observation" is one common ethnographic method in which on ongoing dialogues occur between researchers and participants. Thus, to minimize experimenter bias, researchers are encouraged to take a "stance of ignorance" during interactions. Ethnographic data are particularly useful when research lacks a strong theoretical framework.

As defined in the chapter, epidemiology is the study of the occurrence and distribution of diseases and other health-related conditions in populations. Epidemiology is used more by community psychologists than any other group of psychologists. Two common statistics used in this method are "prevalence" and "incidence." The former refers to the total number of people within a population with a condition; the later refers to the number of individuals within a population who have acquired a condition within a specific time period. Although it is a more inclusive measure and is easier to calculate, prevalence data are harder to interpret since they represent both the incidence and duration of a disorder. A practical example of the epidemiological method using HIV and AIDS is provided by the authors.

Needs assessment is another alternative research method. It refers to a set of approaches which elucidate the magnitude of an issue or examine a set of issues in relation to the available resources for addressing the issues. That is, how much of a problem is there, and what are the available resources for addressing this problems? Needs assessment can be conducted with a variety of methods including ethnographic interviews, surveys, and other descriptive techniques.

After intervention programs have been initiated, their effects need to be evaluated. The authors recommend a four-component program evaluation system, which assesses (a) goals, (b) objectives, (c) activities, and (d) milestones. Still, program evaluators often experience "role ambiguity," especially if they are a staff member of the organization being evaluated. To protect against this, advisory panels often conduct program evaluations rather than a single individual. The authors review several well-known advisory panels (e.g., the Rand Corporation, the Stanford Research International).

VI. A Sense of Urgency!!

Value of Multiple Measures

As discussed in Chapter 1, community psychologists feel the need to study important social issues in a timely manner. That is why more and more studies are using the correlational method (Speer et al., 1992). Of course, this means a lack of experimental control.

One thing researchers can do to increase the validity of their results is to get multiple measures when studying a phenomenon. For example, alcohol usage could be measures in many ways. One method is to simply ask people how much they drink. Unfortunately, people often lie. Therefore, it is useful to have other measures of alcohol usage to validate self-reports. An "unobtrusive measure," such as the number of beer cans in a person's garbage, can serve as a creative alternative index of alcohol consumption.

Unfortunately, different measures of the same behavior often disagree. For example, as indicated in the chapter, one study found that women's self-reported drug consumption did not correspond with their umbilical cord blood specimens. In such cases, researchers must explain for the discrepant findings.

Value of Cultural Sensitivity

Students should be aware of the importance of doing culturally sensitive research--that is, research appreciating intragroup and intergroup differences. Along these lines, the ecological validity of a study can be compromised by research lacking in cultural sensitivity. For example, unskilled White researchers studying a primarily African-American organization might be perceived as being insensitive to certain forces operating within the organization. Thus, program evaluation (like all community research) should strive towards a good "person-environment fit."

Multiple Choice Questions

1. The process of hypothesis testing allows researchers ...
   a. to prove their theories through scientific methods.
   * b. to disconfirm (disprove) the null hypothesis.
   c. to prove the alternative hypothesis.
   d. a guarantee against experimental mortality.

2. Your job is to evaluate a new treatment program for recovering alcoholics. As part of the program, individuals who receive treatment are allowed to share their thoughts about the program with individuals assigned to the control group. Scientifically, this presents which threat to scientific fidelity?
   a. maturation
   * b. diffusion of treatment
   c. experimental mortality
   d. reliability

3. In order to study marijuana usage among American undergraduates, you survey a representative sample of undergraduates from your university. Which of the following best describes your sampling strategy?
   * a. convenience sampling
   b. random sampling
   c. purposive
   d. none of the above

4. The correlation between job stress and alcohol consumption is +0.35. This indicates that ...
   a. Working at a stressful job causes people to drink excessively.
   b. Excessive alcohol consumptions causes people to enter stressful jobs.
   * c. There is a relationship between job stress and alcohol consumption.
   d. All of the above are true.

5. All of the following speak to the fidelity of research except:
   a. reliability
   b. internal validity
   c. external validity
   * d. theory

6. Which of the following statements is (are) true?
   * a. specific human behaviors (e.g., cocaine use) can be described by more than one theory.
   b. Specific theories can only be tested by single models of that theory.
   c. A theory is a blueprint of a model
   d. All of the above are true

7. According to Kuhn (1970) ...
   a. theories change in a linear fashion.
   * b. paradigm changes typically stem from crises within a field.
   c. change within a field is typically predictable.
   d. none of the above is true

8. The goals of a theory include all of the following except...
   a. to predict
   b. to control
   * c. to disprove
   d. to describe

9. In order to study the homeless, you go to various shelters across the United States to interview a random assortment of persons from various backgrounds. You are using which sampling method?
   * a. Random
   b. Convenient
   c. Purposive
   d. none of the above

10. In order to study the homeless, you interview your next-door-neighbor, Ned, who knows several homeless people. You are using which sampling strategy?
    a. Random
    * b. Convenient
    c. Purposive
    d. none of the above

11. In order to study homelessness among Vietnam Veterans, you scan the streets of major Unites States cities looking for homeless persons carrying signs saying, "Vietnam Vet...please spare some money." You are using which sampling strategy?
    a. Random
    b. Convenient
    * c. Purposive
    d. none of the above

12. The _____ causes the _____.
    a. dependent variable; independent variable
    b. operational definition; dependent variable
    * c. independent variable; dependent variable
    d. operational definition; independent & dependent variables.

Questions 13 to 17 utilize the following:
Alcoholics Anonymous (A.A.) claims to help millions of persons quit alcohol use. To test this, you interview 100 persons the day before they start A.A. and then interview them again one year later. The main purpose of your interview is to determine if these 100 individuals are

sober one year after participation. Your interview consists of a single question, "Do you still drink alcohol?" Sobriety is defined as total abstinence from any alcohol.

13. The independent variable in this A.A. study is...
     a. sobriety
   * b. participation in A.A.
     c. Your interview
     d. Alcohol use

14. The dependent variable in this study is...
   * a. alcohol use
     b. participation in A.A.
     c. Your interview
     d. the number of participants who remain in treatment after one year.

15. The operational definition of the dependent variable in this study is ...
     a. alcohol use
   * b. abstinence
     c. participation in A.A.
     d. the number of participants who remain in treatment after one year.

16. Imagine that all the participants in A.A. whom you interview also live together in the same housing facility. This situation would present which threat to treatment fidelity?
     a. compensation
   * b. diffusion of treatment
     c. maturation
     d. experimental mortality

17. Imagine that all the participants in A.A. whom you interview are people who live close to you geographically. This situation would present which threat to treatment fidelity?
   * a. selection bias
     b. compensation
     c. historical events
     d. None of the above present threats to research fidelity

18. Research fidelity refers to all of the following except...
     a. ethics
     b. internal validity
   * c. hypothesis testing
     d. reliability

19. To the extent that any changes in a dependent variable are definitely due to manipulation of the independent variable, a researcher has demonstrated ...
     a. external validity
     b. reliability
     c. confounding effects
   * d. internal validity

20. Your research has clearly demonstrated a relationship between gender and community orientation. That is, women are much more likely than men to work in soup kitchens and volunteer time for crack babies. However, other researchers have failed to find these results. Therefore, your findings and conclusions currently lack ...
* a. reliability
  b. external validity
  c internal validity
  d. ethics

21. Approval from Institutional Review Boards is necessary to assure that research maintains ...
* a. ethics
  b. internal validity
  c. theory
  d. external validity

22. Control is the hallmark of the _____ design.
  a. correlational
* b. experimental
  c. field research
  d. all of the above

23. The Pearson Correlation Coefficient gives information about _____ when describing the relationship between two variables.
  a. magnitude
  b. direction
  c. causality
* d. both a & b

24. Imagine that the correlation between education and drug use is -.59. That is, smarter people are more likely to use drugs. However, further research indicates that both of these variables are caused by a third variable--SES. That is, the relationship between education and drug use is really influenced by a SES. This newer finding suggests that the relationship between education and drug use represents a _____ correlation.
* a. spurious
  b. negative
  c. non-causal
  d. positive

25. Imagine that 100 cocaine addicts were selected for a community-based treatment program. Fifty addicts were assigned to the treatment program. The other fifty received no treatment to serve as a comparison group. The cocaine habits of the 100 cocaine addicts were measured two weeks before beginning the program and then six months after participation in the program. This research utilized which type of methodology?
* a. pretest-posttest control group design
  b. nonequivalent pretest-posttest control group design
  c. field research
  d. correlational methodology

26. In order to determine how much alcohol a person drinks during one week, we have him fill out a questionnaire AND count the number of bar tab receipts in his wallet. This is an example of ...
   a. the experimental method
 * b. multiple methods
   c. systems theory
   d. alternative hypotheses

27. According to past research, about ____ percent of women abuse some form of drugs during pregnancy.
 * a. 15
   b. 25
   c. 50
   d. 75

28. "A _____ is a systematic attempt to explain observable events relating to an issue such as homelessness or alcoholism."
 * a. model
   b. paradigm
   c. theory
   d. dependent variable

29. "A(n) _____ is a working blueprint of a theory."
   a. paradigm
   b. operational definition
   c. independent variable
 * d. model

30. According to Kuhn (1970), a paradigm acts as a(n) _____ for scientific interpretation.
 * a. guide
   b. theoretical standard
   c. operational definition
   d. system

31. "In order to study alcohol abuse, it is important to recruit 'hard core' alcoholics rather than college students who drink a lot." This statement refers to the important issue of ...
   a. operational definitions
 * b. sampling strategies
   c. internal validity
   d. external validity

32. The goal of research is to _____ the null hypothesis.
   a. accept
   b. prove
 * c. reject
   d. all of the above

33. According to your book, participation in research should not endanger people in which of the following ways?
   a. physically
   b. psychologically
   c. socially
 * d. all of the above

34. Which of the following is an example of "compensation?"
   a. Research participants get paid for receiving an experimental drug.
 * b. Research participants assigned to a control group report being more depressed than they actually are because they believe they should be receiving treatment.
   c. Research participants who drop out of treatment prematurely are more likely to be psychologically disturbed than those who remain in treatment.
   d. None of the above

35. The strongest possible correlation between two variables is _____.
   a. -1.00
   b. +1.00
   c. 0
 * d. both a & b are true

36. _____ refers to the extent that concrete or measurable features, or both, of a theory are replicable.
 * a. Reliability
   b. Internal Validity
   c. External validity
   d. Integrity

37. _____ refers to the generalizability of results from a study to other studies or settings.
   a. Reliability
   b. Internal Validity
 * c. External Validity
   d. Integrity

38. _____ refers to the degree to which an independent variable is responsible for any observed changes in a dependent variable.
   a. Reliability
 * b. Internal Validity
   c. External Validity
   d. Integrity

39. The goal of _____ is to describe, predict, and control for why and how variables relate to one another.
 * a. theory
   b. model
   c. independent variable
   d. dependent variable

40. Which research method allows community psychologists to conduct social interactions with research participants?
   a. epidemiology
   b. experimental design
 * c. ethnography
   d. unobtrusive methods

41. Ethnographic research is more commonly used by _____ than _____.
   a. community psychologists; anthropologists
   b. anthropologists; community psychologists
   c. sociologists; community psychologists
 * d. both b & c are true

42. Ethnographic research...
 * a. is useful for yielding qualitative information.
   b. is most useful for research questions driven by a strong theoretical framework.
   c. is used more frequently by community psychologists than sociologists.
   d. discourages participants from answering questions in their own language.

43. Information of prevalence is typically generated from _____, whereas information on incidence is typically generated from _____.
   a. prospective designs; retrospective designs
 * b. retrospective designs; prospective designs
   c. ethnographic designs; experimental designs
   d. retrospective designs; ethnographic designs

44. _____ refers to the study of the occurrence and distribution of diseases and other health-related problems within a population.
   a. Ethnography
   b. Needs assessment
 * c. Epidemiology
   d. None of the above

45. Program evaluation consists of all the following components except ...
   a. goals
   b. objectives
   c. actions
 * d. selection bias

46. To protect against "role ambiguity" when conducting program evaluations, some organizations utilize...
   a. ethnographic interviews
 * b. an advisory panel
   c. a single program evaluator
   d. unobtrusive measures

47. Needs assessment. ...
   a. refers to a set of research methods for evaluating the magnitude of an issue.
   b. examines a set of issues in relation to the available resources for addressing these issues.
   c. can be conducted with a variety of research methods, including ethnography and surveys.
 * d. all of the above are true.

48. The number of undergraduates at your university catching the common cold between June, 1993 and June, 1994 is 25,000. This number represents the _____ of the common cold for this time period.
* a. incidence
  b. prevalence
  c. operationalization
  d. reliability

Identification of Terms

1. Blueprint of a theory. (Answer= model).

2. Sampling strategy in which participants are chosen because they are easily available. (Answer=convenient).

3. Assumption that results are due solely to chance or random error. (Answer= null hypothesis).

4. Discontinuation of participants in experiment or treatment (Answer= experimental mortality).

5. The generalizability of results from a study to other studies or settings. (Answer = external validity).

6. An experimental design involving the assessment of effects both prior to and following an experimental manipulation in one group but not another. (Answer = pretest-posttest control group design).

7. A systematic attempt to explain observable events relating to an issue. (Answer= theory).

8. A systematic plan to test out an hypothesis. (answer= design)

9. Ethics, reliability, external validity, and internal validity comprise what concept? (Answer = research fidelity).

10. The research method yielding a Pearson Correlation Coefficient. (Answer= correlational).

Food for Thought

I. Imagine the following situation. Los Angeles courts have mandated that 100 drug abusing, Caucasian males from the community participate in a drug treatment program. The goal of the program is to get these males to stop drug abuse. The 100 males all begin "Project Anti-drug," a six week program.

Over the six week period, 65 males drop out of the study. However, among the 35 individuals who complete the program, 32 report to the courts that they have greatly reduced their drug use. Only three report that they did not change their drug consumption.

Based on these findings, the L.A. courts conclude that "Project Anti-drug" is an effective program to combat drug abuse and should be universally implemented for all drug users.

Question: What are the scientific problems with the court's conclusion? Specifically, address the issue of research fidelity. Which threats to research fidelity have been violated? Why? BE SPECIFIC!!

II. Imagine that you've developed your own theory of child abuse. Your theory states that financially deprived (low SES) parents engage in more child abuse than affluent parents due to greater financial pressures. How could you test this theory? Indicate the research methods and sampling strategies you would use, as well as possible deseign flaws and problems in interpretation.

[Answer notes: Here are some possibilities:
(a) Using questionnaires, interview a random sample of parents about how much they physically punish their children. Also ask them their SES. Assess the correlation between SES and physical punishment of children.
    Method = Correlational Method
    Sampling = Random

(b) Bring child abusing and non-child abusing parents into the laboratory for an experiment. In the experiment parents are exposed to a noxious stimulus (loud, uncontrollable noise). Measure how many times the parents punch the table <u>before</u> and <u>after</u> hearing the noxious stimulus.
    Method= Quasi-experimental (non-equivalent pretest-posttest design)
    Sampling= Purposive

(c) Place a video-camera in homes where child abuse has been reported. Record parent-child interactions to see if these parents are more likely to curse at their children on days when bills are sent to the house.
    Method= Field Study (and correlational method)
    Sampling= Purposive

III. How would you operationally define the following terms? (Be creative!):

Term	Possible definitions
(a) Alcohol Abuse	-- drinking to point where alcohol interferes with job functioning? --more than six drinks per day? --high score on the Michigan Alcohol Screening Test (MAST)?
(b) Child Abuse	--physically smacking a child more than three times per day? --verbal attacks which cause a child to cry? --Any behavior(s) which violate state laws?
(c) Depression	--Negative feelings and thoughts which prevent a person from rising and dressing in the morning?

--High scores on the Beck Depression
Inventory?
--Depletion of serotonin at neural synapses?

IV. You believe that you have developed a superior treatment program for depression. You think that it is a special program that will work for all types of depressed persons, even the severe cases. To test the effectiveness of this intervention, you recruit 60 African American undergraduates from your university to participate in your 10-week program. Of the 60 students, 10 live by themselves off campus and 50 live in the same dormitory on campus.

Thirty-five students complete the entire program. Results indicate that all 35 students are cured of depression. You conclude that your program is a total success and should be used to treat depression.

What is wrong with this conclusion? What threats to research fidelity limit this conclusion?

[Answer note: Possible answers:
(a) Selection Bias-- Only African American undergraduates were selected for this study.

(b) Diffusion of Treatment--50 students lived in the same dormitory and may have influenced one another.

(c) Experimental Mortality--25 participants dropped out of the program.

(d) Maturation/History--Subjects were all undergraduates and, for the most part, represented a single cohort.

Key Terms

Acquired immunodeficiency syndrome
Activity
Alternative hypothesis
Analysis
Client compensate
Confounding effects
Constituent validity
Consultant
Consultees
Convenience sample
Correlational methods
Cultural sensitivity
Dependent variable
Design
Diffusion of treatment
Epidemiology
Ethnics
Ethnography
Experimental method
Experimental mortality
External validity
Field research
Goal
Human immunodeficiency virus
Hypothesis testing
Incidence
Independent variable
Institute review board
Internal validity
Logical positivism
Maturation
Measurement
Milestone
Model
Multiple Methods
Needs assessment
Nonequivalent pretest-posttest control design
Null hypothesis
Objective
Operational definition
Outcome measures
Paradigm
Participant observation
Pearson Correlation Coefficient
Pretest-posttest control group design
Prevalence
Process measures
Program evaluation
Prospective design
Purposive sample
Quasi-experimental design
Random assignment
Random sample
Reliability

Retrospective design
Sampling strategies
Selection bias
Spurious association
System
Systems theory
Theory
Unobtrusive measure

Recommended Films

<u>Two Research Styles</u> (24 minutes). Profiling two styles of psychological research, this program examines research methodology and design. Examples are provided from Dr. Chris Alford's research on alcohol consumption and daily activities. Insight Media. 2162 Broadway, New York, New York, 10024. Fax: 212-799-5309

CHAPTER 3

THE IMPORTANCE OF SOCIAL CHANGE

Introduction

This chapter reviews the reasons why social change occurs as well as the methods by which they occur. Students are introduced to a number of factors: diverse populations, declining resources, accountability, knowledge-based and technological changes, community conflict, dissatisfaction with traditional services, and desire for diversity of solutions. Two types of social change, unplanned/spontaneous and planned, are also reviewed. The authors emphasize the importance of action research and program evaluation to assess the effects of social change efforts.

Lectures and Notes

I. Background: From Individual to Community/Government Reliance

The Great Depression was a drastic period of change for many reasons. Some of these changes would ultimately have strong implications for community psychologists. Prior to the Great Depression, individual community members were more reliant upon themselves and immediate neighbors during times of crisis. Individuals would team up with an impressive display of crisis management and resourceful coping. After the Great Depression, individuals became more dependent on formal community services and government aid for assistance. This was a major social change in the history of psychology.

Community psychologists are interested in studying the various dimensions of social change: Why does it occur? Can we predict it? Can we cope with it? How can we direct it? As mentioned in Chapter 1, a multidisciplinary approach is most useful for a comprehensive understanding of social change.

II. Reasons For Social Change

Diverse Populations. Our society contains a variety of diverse groups, each with its own problems and needs. Think about AIDS, cancer, teen pregnancy, drunk driving, and unemployment, just to name a few examples. Each has its own needs which might not be met by society.

For example, persons with lower incomes are discouraged from voting due to transportation difficulties, inaccessibility, or the lack of a home address. Fawcett et al. (1988) tried to increase voter registration by providing food and other commodities at registration sites for families at less than 125% of the federal poverty line. This manipulation resulted in a 100% increase in the actual number of voter registrants and a 51% increase in the actual number of voters in presidential elections.

Individual groups often self-motivate, organize, and fight for their own social rights. One example cited in the chapter is the Gray Panthers, an organization fighting for the rights of the elderly.

<u>Declining Resources.</u> Most community service programs are dependent upon external funding sources, such as the government, as well as grants from public or private endowments or foundations. In other words, diverse groups must compete with one another for scarce resources. And because "demonstration" programs are risky and require tremendous time lags, funding often goes to traditional groups. There has been a "Robin Hood in reverse" effect (Delgado, 1986), with fewer monies going to human services.

Popular private foundations include the Ford Foundation, the Charles Stewart Foundation, The Henry J. Kaiser Foundation, and the Robert Wood Johnson Foundation. Agencies often charge on a "sliding scale," that is, fees are determined by income and number of dependents. Unfortunately, the call for monies by disenfranchised groups is often matched by threats from angry taxpayers who do not want their taxes raised.

Major corporations are becoming socially conscious. For example, Ben and Jerry's Ice Cream Inc. donate 7.5% of its pretax income to diverse charities, such as the preservation of the Amazon Rain Forest. Former President Jimmy Carter also started the Atlanta Project, which has gotten Delta Air Lines and Coco Cola involved in community affairs.

<u>Accountability</u>. According to the chapter, accountability is the obligation to account for or be responsible for transactions, monetary or otherwise. "Cost effectiveness" means that monies should be spent wisely. Everybody wants both accountability and cost effectiveness today.

<u>Knowledge-based and technological change.</u> Our society has been experiencing a technological explosion in recent years. However, not everybody feels comfortable with these changes. For example, a recent survey of 500 California residents revealed high levels of "technophobia" (Pilisuk & Acredolo, 1988). Specifically, respondents were concerned about contaminated drinking water, cancer, nuclear accidents, polluted air, and endangered food and transportation. Women, minority groups, and the less educated were the most fearful.

<u>Community Conflict.</u> When diverse groups come together because of conflict, broad-based changes may result. One example within psychology was the emergency of the American Psychological Association. Another example is the field of mediation, which grew out of efforts to reduce racial tensions in Rochester, New York during the 1960's.

<u>Dissatisfaction With Traditional Services.</u>

<u>Desire For Diverse Solutions.</u> When community members are dissatisfied with existent options, they often demand change. For example, an alternative to the traditional legal system was implemented in Washington, D.C. Specifically, a "multi-door" legal approach was implemented in which citizens were informed about the various legal options available to them. This approach helps to reduce bureaucracy.

III. Types of Social Change

<u>Spontaneous or Unplanned Change.</u> Examples include natural disasters (e.g., earthquakes, floods, fires) as well as generational issues. For example, as baby boomers get older and require greater community services, society must prepare to deal with this problem. Furthermore, baby boomers must contend with the needs of their own children as well as their aging parents, thus rendering them the "sandwich generation." High divorce rates, single parent families, and blended families are other examples.

Unplanned change is often stressful because it is (a) serious, (b) uncontrollable, and (c) often occurring in novel environments where we least expect or prepare for it.

Community psychologists try to predict spontaneous change so that people can better prepare to cope with it. Census data are often useful for predicting changes. For example, given the large number of baby boomers, we can expect a dramatic increase in the needs for the elderly in the future. Social indicators are also useful for prediction. Finally, when attempt to make predictions for the future, the "base-rate problem" must be addressed. For example, although we may be quick to identify someone as schizophrenic based on bizarre behavioral patterns, we must remember that schizophrenia is very rare in the general population and that most people who talk to themselves are not schizophrenic!

<u>Planned Social Change</u>. Planned change is intentional, directed, and purposive. Specifically, it is characterized by four elements:

* it is limited in scope (that is, it is focused).
* it is directed towards enhancing the life of community members.
* it offers new roles to those affected by change.
* it is often guided by a person who acts as a change agent (typically a professional, but sometimes advocates from client groups, political activists, or educations experts).

There are numerous planned change strategies, including:
* grass roots activism.
* networking of services.
* social support.
* external consultants.
* educational and informational programs.
* public policy processes.

<u>Issues Related To Planned Change:</u>

a. <u>Who should initiate change</u>? Experts disagree on who is the "best" person to initiate change. Some believe that administrators and managers should begin the process. Others believe that change is more likely to occur when started by those at the bottom of the organization, including staff, clients, and other lay persons.

b. <u>Is collaboration good?</u> Yes. Community psychologists universally agree that social scientists and clients should work together to initiate change. This process is also called "participatory decision-making" or "collaborative problem solving." Collaboration is one key to empowerment and self-determination.

c. Do planned changes last? Not always. For example, Prestby & Wandersman (1985) found that 50% of the voluntary neighborhood associations which they sampled became inactive after only one year. Furthermore, in order for change to last, multifactedted and continuous efforts are needed. "Once and for all" solutions usually fail.

d. What are the best kinds of change?

* Changes should be humanitarian, allowing for individuals and groups to actualize their full potential.
* Change should be problem-focused.
* Change should be feasible and practical, while trying to reach as many groups as possible.
* Plans for change should be "pluralistic"--focusing on the environments in which change will occur.

IV. Why Change Plans Fail

Resistance is one major reason why change efforts fail. Some individuals within a group believe in tradition, perceiving it as safe or superior. New ideas are often perceived as threatening and risky. Some people rigidly espouse old approaches and will not listen to alternative ideas. Some individuals are dogmatic. Other people resist change because they are too lazy to think critically about new approaches. These individuals, called "cognitive misers," exert minimal effort when making decisions or problem-solving.

Social movements frequently fail when they become overly focused on a single issue which does not appeal to enough groups. For this reason, the March of Dimes abandoned its sole focus on polio to include all other birth defects.

Radical approaches to social change often fail. Despite claims that such tactics work, agitation often invites negative media attention which hurts change efforts. Alinsky (1971) outlined his approach to confrontative but effective change:

* Use whatever you've got to get attention.
* Ridicule is a potent weapon which makes the opposition react to your advantage.
* Don't let your tactics drag on too long.
* Chose a tactic which your people like.
* Keep the pressure on.

Planned change often fails due to a lack of organizational infrastructure. Maton (1988) found that groups with higher role differentiation, greater organization and order, and more capable leaders reported more positive well-being and positive group appraisal.

Finally, conducting systematic research is a good safeguard against program failure. Theory-driven "action research" is useful for monitoring problems as they arise during the process of change and for indicating when strategy modifications are necessary. Program evaluation is also important.

Multiple Choice Questions

1. According to the authors, current industrial societies are...
   a. more self-reliant than past societies.
   b. less cooperative than past societies in resolving social problems.
   * c. more dependent on government services than past societies.
   d. less dependent on community services than past societies.

2. Ever since _____, citizens within the United States have been more dependent on external agencies during crises.
   * a. the Great Depression
   b. the initiation of the Carnegie Foundation
   c. the initiation of the McArthus Foundation
   d. the initiation of the American Arbitration Association

3. According to psychologist Leigh Marlowe (1971), the rate of social change has been ...
   a. unimpressive
   b. tailing off after years of rapid acceleration
   c. declining since the advent of arbitration and mediation
   * d. accelerating

4. Community psychologists are interested in which of the following questions regarding social change?
   a. how can change be predicted?
   b. what causes change?
   c. how to best cope with change?
   * d. all of the above

5. Which of the following is not a reason for social change?
   a. declining resources
   * b. similar populations
   c. increased accountability
   d. desire for diverse solutions to problems.

6. Fawcett, Seekins, and Silber (1988) implemented an intervention to increase voter registration and turn-out using food incentives. The authors found that their intervention...
   a. increased voter registration but not actual voter turn-out.
   * b. increased both voter registration and actual voter turn-out.
   c. increased neither voter registration nor voter turn-out.
   d. increased voter turn-out and voter registration among middle class participants only.

7. Using food incentives to increase voter turn-out and registration among the poor, Fawcett, Seekins, and Silber (1988) found that their intervention...
   * a. increased voter registration more than voter turn-out.
   b. increased voter turn-out and registration equally.
   c. increased neither voter turn-out or registration.
   d. actually decreased voter registration.

8. The organization concerned with the rights of the elderly is called...
   * a. The Grey Panthers
   b. The Black Panthers
   c. The Maggie Kuhn Forum
   d. both b & c are true.

9. Imagine that you just started your own community service program to reduce discrimination in your neighborhood. You want to get funding for your program. In all probability, your program is least likely to be...
   a. dependent on the government for funding
   * b. self-sufficient
   c. dependent on public or private foundations for money
   d. competing against other organizations for funds.

10. You organize a community "demonstration" program to reduce teen pregnancies. Unfortunately, efforts to procure funding for your new program will be stifled by ...
   a. reduced federal funds
   b. reduced local funds
   c. the "Robin Hood in Reverse Effect"
   * d. all of the above

11. Which of the following is not a funding agency...
   a. The Henry J. Kaiser Foundation.
   * b. The Reagan Federation
   c. The McArthur Foundation
   d. The Robert Wood Johnson Foundation

12. You go see a therapist whose fees are determined by how much money you make and the number of your dependents. This type of payment system is known as...
   a. an accountability system
   * b. a sliding scale
   c. the multi-door approach
   d. all of the above

13. Which of the following organizations have actively contributed money to efforts to preserve the Amazon Rain Forest?
   * a. Ben and Jerry's
   b. Baskin Robbins
   c. TCBY yogurt
   d. both a & c

14. _____ means that monies should be spent wisely.
   a. Accountability
   * b. Cost effectiveness
   c. Sliding scale
   d. all of the above

15. Imagine that you now run the finances for your organization. According to the book, which of the following individuals will hold you accountable for your actions?
    a. staff
    b. licensing bureaus
    c. clients
 * d. all of the above

16. Technological changes in recent years are best described as
    a. "slowing"
 * b. "galloping"
    c. "accelerating"
    d. "plateauing"

17. Pilisuk and Acredolo (1988) studied the people most likely to experience technophobia in California. Based on their findings, which of the following groups would not experience discomfort with the proliferation of new technologies?
 * a. educated individuals
    b. women with limited education
    c. black males
    d. individuals with limited exposure to new technologies

18. Based on Pilisuk and Acredolo's (1988) research on technophobia, which of the following individuals would experience the most anxiety about working with computers?
    a. Peter, whose computer has continuously broken down on him in the past.
 * b. Robin, who has never worked with computers in the past.
    c. David, who is a perfectionist about his computer work.
    d. Ellen, who recently spent $7,000 on an new computer system.

19. Conflict among psychologists led many individuals to leave the _____ and join the _____.
 * a. American Psychological Association; American Psychological Society
    b. American Psychological Society; American Psychological Association
    c. American Psychological Association; American Arbitration Association
    d. none of the above

20. Which of the following fields/organizations emerged as a result of a racial conflict in Rochester, New York?
    a. The American Arbitration Association
    b. community mediation
    c. the American Psychological Society
 * d. more than one of the above is correct

21. You want to create a new, controversial sex education program within your school system. Which of the following individuals is most likely to support your efforts?
   a. Ron, who is satisfied with the current system but thinks change will be needed in a few years.
   b. Linda, who agreed to join your program because she is a long-time friend but likes the current system.
* c. Dean, who dislikes the current system.
   d. Ed, who has vast sexual experience.

22. A multi-door approach to litigation has been tested in Washington, D.C., in order to reduce common bureaucratic hang-ups. This approach includes all of the following except...
   a. volunteer attorneys
   b. mediation/arbitration
* c. monies from funding agencies
   d. assistance from legal aid offices.

23. Baby boomers, having been part of _____ social change, are often referred to as the _____.
   a. planned; sandwich generation.
   b. planned; blended generations
* c. unplanned; sandwich generation
   d. unplanned; blended generation

24. According to research by Bab & Austin (1989), which of the following individuals would be most fearful of crime?
   a. Ed, who was mugged one year ago.
* b. Paul, who lives next to an abandoned building.
   c. Carol, who lives in a wealthy neighborhood with little crime.
   d. Donald, who works on the police force.

25. Unplanned change is typically ...
   a. controllable
* b. rare
   c. uncontained and spread out
   d. not very serious

26. <u>Megatrends 2000</u> presents content analyses of the print media used to forecast upcoming trends.
   a. True
* b. False

27. Cost effectiveness can be defined as the obligation to account for or be responsible for various transactions, monetary or otherwise.
   a. True
* b. False

28. Planned change is typically all of the following except:
* a. broad in scope
   b. led by a change agent
   c. directed towards life enhancement
   d. providing roles for those involved in change.

29. Which of the following is not a change agent:
    a. educational experts
    b. political scientists
    c. advocates from client groups.
  * d. all of the above are change agents

30. Scientists and clients often work together in a process known as either _____ or _____.
  * a. participatory decision-making; collaborative problem solving
    b. joint accountability; collaboration
    c. collaboration; the multi-door approach
    d. participatory decision-making; unplanned change

31. Your boss calls you a "cognitive miser." What does this mean?
    a. it means that you are dogmatic in your thinking
    b. it means that you never change your mind, no matter how much you think about an issue
  * c. it means that you don't like to think about issues
    d. all of the above

32. People who rigidly hold on to their views are called...
  * a. dogmatic
    b. cognitive misers
    c. anti-change agents
    d. all of the above

33. To be successful, planned changes must be ...
    a. humane
    b. feasible
    c. pluralistic
  * d. all of the above

34. You organize a community program to raise money for cancer research. To maximize the success of your organization, your program should ideally ...
    a. target funds for breast cancer only, because it is so common
    b. target funds for liver cancer only, because it is so deadly.
  * c. target funds for all types of cancer, including both liver and breast cancers.
    d. target funds only using professional change agents.

35. According to Alinsky (1971), confrontative change efforts
    a. should use ridicule
    b. do whatever it takes to get public attention
    c. should convey a strong threat.
  * d. all of the above

36. Interactive social relationships established between individuals or organizations are useful for the sharing of information, resources, and other support. This is known as ...
  * a. networking
    b. action research
    c. planned change
    d. all of the above

37. Based on research by Maton (1988), organizations are most satisfied when...
   * a. they have capable leaders
   b. different workers have similar roles and tasks to perform
   c. there is a moderate amount of disorganization.
   d. both a and b are true

38. Which of the following is not a problem with conducting action research...
   a. random assignment of subjects to conditions
   b. trust issues between researchers and community members
   c. negotiating difficulties with community administrators
   * d. all of the above are problems with action research.

39. Both Illinois and Yugoslavia have implemented seat-belt laws. Illinois residents have demonstrated ____ public opposition in response to the law, while Yugoslavian residents demonstrated _____ compliance.
   a. less; less
   * b. more; more
   c. more; less
   d. less; more

40. Program evaluation can be defined as scientific work grounded in theory but directed toward resolving problems.
   a. True
   * b. False

Identification of Terms

1. Professionals or paraprofessionals (e.g., client advocates or educational experts) who induce social change. (Answer=Change agents).

2. Term for individuals who are close-minded, or excessively rigid, in their thinking. (Answer=Dogmatic).

3. A coordinated system for helping citizens work with a bureaucratic legal system. Washington, D.C. established such a system. (Answer=Multidoor approach).

4. Excessive fear of technical advances. (Answer=Technophobia).

5. Type of payment system in which the fee is determined by income and the number of dependents. (Answer=Sliding scale).

6. Phrase meaning that monies should be spent wisely and that profits should accrue. (Answer=Cost effective).

7. The obligation to account for, or be responsible for, business transactions and monies. (Answer=Accountability).

8. People who exert no effort in their thinking and decision-making. (Answer=Cognitive misers).

9. Theoretically-grounded, scientific work directed towards solving social problems. (Answer=action research).

10. Term for a cohort (generation) which lives at home with both their older parents and their children.
(Answer=sandwich generation).

Food For Thought

I. Imagine that you were sent to a new planet, Planet X, where there was never any desire for social change. When you talk to the citizens, you discover extreme satisfaction on Planet X. Based on this observation, what predictions would you make about life on Planet X in terms of (a) the diversity of its population, (b) the distribution of its resources, (c) reaction to technological changes, and (d) voting practices. Make specific predictions and cite studies to support your reasoning.

[Answer notes: Answer should reflect population similarity, equality of resources, ability to cope with technological change, and high voter turn-out.]

II. Give an example of an unplanned social change which occurred in your own life. How would things have differed if this had been a planned social change? Why do people in general respond more negatively to unplanned social change?

III. You attempt to overthrow and remove the President of your college class because you believe that she is incompetent. You organize some friends and execute some "plans for change." Unfortunately, your plans fail drastically. List four factors which might have caused your revolution to change. Consider elements such as the quality of your plan, your friends, and other variables. Cite studies to justify your answer.

IV. President Bill Clinton stirred up much controversy with his push for health care reform in America. His proposal has triggered both strong support and strong opposition. In essence, this system would provide free medical care to all citizens, even for the most expensive medical procedures.
   a. What social forces/conditions have pushed President Clinton to propose this major social change? Relate your answer to the materials and specific studies discussed in the chapter.

[Answer notes: There is much room for creativity here. However, answers should include the greater diversity of people in America; vast technological advances are occurring and making many people feel alienated; community conflict (e.g., racial tensions)]

   b. Why have certain forces opposed this proposal? And if the plan ultimately fails, what conditions would have caused this defeat? Draw on material covered in the chapter.

[Answer notes: pressures from big business such as the American Medical Association; cognitive misers and dogmatic individuals; feeling of alienation by upper class who are happy with their health care coverage;

poor political networking by the President.]

Key Terms

Accountability
Action research
Base rate problem
Blended families
Change agents
Cognitive misers
Collaborative problem solving
Community conflict
Community mediation
Cost effectiveness
Dogmatic (personality)
Induced change
In-group
Knowledge-based change
Mediator
Multi-door courthouse
Networking
Out-group
Participatory decision making
Planned change
Sandwich generation
Sliding scale
Social indicators
Spontaneous social change
Technological change
Technophobia
Unplanned social change

Recommended Films

Fighting For Our Lives (29 minutes). Women constitute the fastest growing group of people with AIDS in the United States. This program focuses on how women are taking action in their own communities to reduce the spread of AIDS among women. Women Make Movies, Inc. 426 Broadway--Suite 500, New York, New York, 10013. Fax: 212-925-2052.

Homeless Not Helpless: Opening Doors (44 minutes). This film explores a variety of programs for empowering homeless persons, including inner-city storefront missions, government social service agencies, and the Union of the Homeless. University of California Extension Center for Media and Independent Learning. 2176 Shattuck Ave., Berkeley, CA, 94704. Fax: 510-643-8683.

Recording the American Experience (25 minutes). This program provides insights into the changing nature of work and why Chicago is still a working class town. California Working Group, Inc. P.O. Box 10326, Oakland, CA 94610-0326.

CHAPTER 4

CREATING AND SUSTAINING SOCIAL CHANGE

<u>Introduction</u>

This chapter introduces students to the various methods of initiating and sustaining social change, including citizen participation, networking, education and information dissemination, and public policy. Advantages and disadvantages of each method are discussed.

<u>Lecture and Notes</u>

<u>I. Creating Planned Change</u>

<u>Citizen Participation</u>

Citizen participation can be broadly defined as involvement in any organized activity in which the individual participates without pay in order to achieve a common goal. Citizen participation has other names including grass roots activism, empowerment, and self-help or mutual assistance groups.

There are various settings for citizen participation including:
* work settings
* architectural environments
* neighborhood associations
* public policy arenas
* education programs
* situations applying science and technology

However, not everybody wants to be involved in social change. One study by O'Neill et al., (1988) examined the extent to which two variables, locus-of-control and perceived world-justice, would predict participation in social change efforts. The authors found that neither variable itself predicted social activism. However, the two variables together did predict social activism. Thus, people with a sense of personal power and the belief that the world is unjust were more likely to be social activists.

Some people want to become socially involved, but lack more sophisticated skills (e.g., lobbying or doing research). It is essential to find some role for these individuals. A process known as <u>team building</u> is often helpful. Team building helps a group to define its goals, analyze tasks and the way tasks are performed, and to examine the relationship among people doing the work.

Of course, another problem is obtaining funding. Most community citizens are unskilled in grant writing.

There are several advantages to citizen participation:
a) Active participants are usually highly motivated and committed to the cause.
b) They are also more knowledgeable about the issues at hand.
c) There is stronger sense of community.

The disadvantages to this method include:
a) Not all community members want to participate.
b) Results often take a long time to be met.
c) Community members with the most motivation and dedication are more likely to experience burnout.
d) If socially active community members are not representative of the larger community (e.g., demographically or socially), nonproductive subgrouping might emerge within the community.

Zinobar and Dinkel (1981) developed a manual to guide individuals interested in participant-induced change. They recommend the social activists make (1) specific suggestions, (2) give specific reasons why change is needed, and (3) obtain a lot of media coverage.

Networking

Networks offer continuous support to community agencies, use reciprocity to share ideas and resources, use modeling for each other, and provide accessible resources to participants. There are various networking organizations:

(a) Enabling systems--vehicles whereby multiple community initiatives can be simultaneously mobilized, supported, and sustained in an efficient manner by developing specific links among social actors.

(b) Networks--Confederations or alliances of related community organizations or individuals. Members usually share funds, information, and ideas.

(c) Umbrella Organizations--Overarching organizations that oversee the health of member organizations. They can act as information clearing houses.

(d) Community development corporations and neighborhood associations--Citizen groups which come together to conquer social problems.

(e) Clearinghouse--Umbrella organizations which individuals can contract for assistance in finding appropriate self-help groups.

The advantages of umbrella organizations include:
(a) They promote interaction and collaboration between supportive systems.

(b) They can ensure equitable distribution of resources.

(c) They reduce community conflict.

(d) They identify cracks in the system.

The disadvantages of umbrella organizations include:
(a) Private agencies might feel threatened by more powerful networks and try to rebel against them.

(b) Networks might become overcontrolling or overparenting with smaller agencies.

(c) Organizations might have problems coordinating the efforts of community organizations which are at different stages of developmental.

(d) If certain associations grow too large and expansive, other associations in neighboring communities might feel threatened and might try to subvert progress.

Professional Change Agents

A consultant is someone who engages in collaborative problem-solving with one or more persons (the <u>consultees</u>) who are responsible for providing some form of assistance to another third person (the <u>client</u>). Despite the challenges of utilizing consultants, they do help. Medway and Updyke (1985) compared organizations that either used, or did not use, consultants. They found that consultees and clients showed positive gains on several outcome measures, including attitudinal scales, overt behavior, and standardized scores.

The advantages of using consultants include:
(a) Consultants are experts.
(b) Because they are neutral, consultants can make unencumbered and unbiased recommendations.
(c) Consultants generally take a long-term approach to problem-solving.
(d) Consultants have vast experience with similar problems.

The disadvantages of using consultants include:
(a) Consultants can be costly to an organization.
(b) Outside consultants sometimes inspire fear, defensiveness, and resistance to change.
(c) Consultants usually have time-limited contacts with clients.
(d) Clients might hold unrealistically high expectations of consultants.

Education and Information Dissemination

Successful community programs and research findings are useless unless they can be disseminated to others. Indeed, education and information dissemination can save lots of time, money, and effort. This information can be used both to shape ideology and direct community action. The main purpose of information dissemination is to improve the community, to promote prevention in favor of treatment, and to empower community members.

Unfortunately, information dissemination has received little attention in the community psychology literature. Also, certain educational messages will not be received by the targeted audience.

Fairweather and Davidson (1986) suggest two factors which explain failure: (a) personal characteristics of the adaptor (e.g., dogmatic individuals), and (b) characteristics of the social context (e.g., groups content with the status quo).

In order to be effective, education dissemination needs to be evaluated with multiple outcome measures. For example, Seitz et al. (1991) evaluated the effectiveness of an intervention targeting pregnant teenagers. They measured various outcomes including drop out rates, failing grades, vocational activities, and grade point average.

Education dissemination also needs to be culturally sensitive. That is, what works for one ethnic group might not work for another one. For example, Marin et al. (1992) tested a media-based community intervention designed to increase knowledge about cigarette smoking and to introduce culturally-appropriate cessation services. However, results indicated that change was greatest among the less acculturated Hispanics.

The advantages of education and information-dissemination include:
(a) The capacity to reach a large and diverse audience.
(b) Education is generally revered in America.
(c) It is a relatively inexpensive form of social change.

The disadvantages of education and information-dissemination include:
(a) Information will have no effects on some individuals.
(b) Information has to be custom designed for its audience.
(a) Sometimes the effects of information-dissemination are not what community psychologists plan for. For example, Prince-Embury (1992) provided educational and health information to residence surrounding Three Mile Island after a nuclear accident. Although stress declined shortly after the literature dissemination, many respondents reported less perceived control! This was not intended by the researcher.

Public Policy

Public policy can refer to a policy at a specific agency or at the level of local, state, and federal government. Public policy can also influence money allocations. The aim of public policy is to improve the quality of life for community members. "Policy Science," a related concept, is the science of making findings from science relevant to governmental and organizational policy.

One important question is how much scientific findings should influence public policy. Some argue that public policy should only be guided by documented scientific findings. However, it often takes many years to get good scientific data. Therefore, some argue that public policy on pressing issues such as AIDS and homelessness should not have to wait until an entire armament of data are accumulated. Unfortunately, public policy frequently is not guided by data, humanitarianism, or logical thinking. Rather, political pressures, lobbying groups, and popular public concerns often dictate the law. Media attention also directs public policy, which is why the media are accused of agenda setting.

Public policy serves several functions:
(a) Instrumental Purpose--Occurs when research shapes the direction of change or public policy.
(b) Conceptual Purpose--Occurs when research shapes the way people think and conceptualize social problems and solutions.
(c) Persuasive Purpose--Occurs when research persuades policy makers to support a particular position on a social problem.
(d) Predictive Purpose--Occurs when research is used to predict social change in the future and to estimate whether change efforts will be successful.

Indeed, there is evidence that policy makers, such as legislators, are influenced by research findings. Even Trudy Vincent (1990) drew parallels for members of Congress and community psychologists. That is, both attend to the people, settings, events, and histories of districts before establishing policy.

Community psychologists and community members can influence lawmakers in several ways:
(a) Lobbying--That is, to direct pressure at public officials to promote the passage of particular legislation or policy.
(b) Seek elected offices.
(c) Amicus Curiae--"Friend of the court." For example, Susan Fiske was an amicus curiae in Price Waterhouse v. Hopkins, a court case dealing with gender stereotyping.
(d) Guide to advocacy in the public interest, developed by the American Psychological Association.
(d) Public Interest Directorate--prepared by the American Psychological Association, which advances and disseminates to government offices information relating to applied human welfare.

The advantages of public policy include:
(a) The potential to initiate broad sweeping changes.
(b) The average American has considerable respect for the law and will honor changes in law.
(c) Policy makers often have a broad perspective and understanding of community needs and dynamics.

The disadvantages of public policy include:
(a) Some researchers are motivated to promote their own careers ("publish or perish") rather than to initiate social change.
(b) Some researchers are perceived by community members as agents of a traditional, oppressive system which is not interesting in change.
(c) Voter turn-out is biased. The individuals most effected by legislation often cannot, or do not, vote on these policies.
(d) Policy making can be a very slow, laborious, and politicized process.

Multiple Choice Questions

1. Which of the following is NOT an alternative label for "citizen participation?"
   a. grass roots activism
 * b. umbrella organization
   c. self-help
   d. empowerment

2. Some psychologists prefer the term _____ instead of self-help group.
   a. umbrella network
   b. social allegiance
   c. public assistance
 * d. mutual assistance

3. Alan believes that the world is unfair and that change is virtually impossible. Bob believes that the world is fair and that change is still possible. Carl believes that the world is mostly unfair, but that changes for the better are possible. According to research by O'Neill et al. (1988), which person is most likely to be a social activist?
   a. Alan
   b. Bob
 * c. Carl
   d. Both Bob and Carl are equally likely to be social activists.

4. Which of the following is generally considered to be the best measure of the impact of citizen participation?
   a. cost savings
   b. increased profits
   c. higher client satisfaction
  * d. there is no agreement on what is the "best" measure of citizen impact

5. Which of the following statements about citizen participation is true?
   a. successful outcomes are usually defined in terms of increased profits
   b. successful outcomes are usually defined in terms of higher client satisfaction.
  * c. there is no general consensus on what is the "best" measure of successful outcome.
   d. citizen participation rarely has successful outcomes.

6. In human service settings, which individuals are most likely to experience burnout?
  * a. those with the highest dedication.
   b. those with the most social support.
   c. those not belonging to mutual support groups.
   d. those who have been in the organization the longest.

7. Citizen participation is more likely to fail if...
   a. results come too quickly.
  * b. the costs to change outweigh the benefits.
   c. a small group of activists is seen as very similar to and representative of the larger affected community.
   d. both b and c are true.

8. _____ are vehicles whereby multiple community initiatives can be simultaneously mobilized, supported, and sustained in an efficient manner by developing specified links among the social actors.
   a. Consultant contracts
  * b. Enabling Systems
   c. Clearinghouses
   d. Pro bono work agreements

9. According to Weed (1990), the first step for community psychologists working as consultants is to...
   a. introduce the new research or program
   b. raise the awareness of the individuals in the setting under consultation
  * c. define the goals to be accomplished
   d. measure baseline (before intervention) observations

10. Many institutionalized populations, such as the mentally ill or disabled, are being moved back into the community in a process called _____.
   a. reinstitutionalization
   b. institutionalization decenterment
  * c. deinstitutionalization
   d. community replacement

11. Thom Wolff described community services for mentally ill as being _____
    a. well-integrated
    b. unnecessary
  * c. fragmented and poorly organized
    d. inconsistent with the community psychology model

12. According to the chapter, information disseminators should be thought of as _____.
    a. dictators
  * b. collaborators
    c. umbrella organizations
    d. consultants

13. Which of the following is an advantage of information dissemination methods?
    a. a wide audience can be reached
    b. education is generally revered in the United States
    c. it is relatively inexpensive compared to other methods of social change
  * d. all of the above are advantages of information dissemination

14. _____ aim(s) to directly improve the quality of life for community members.
    a. Clearinghouses
  * b. Public policy
    c. Consultants
    d. Amicus curiae

15. The _____ has the mission of advancing the scientific and professional aspects of psychology as applied to human welfare and disseminating reports to state and federal governments and legislators.
    a. Supreme Court
  * b. Public Interest Directorate of the A.P.A.
    c. Amicus curiae
    d. consultee

16. The purpose of lobbying is to ...
    a. disseminate information
    b. direct individuals towards appropriate self-help groups
    c. provide social support
  * d. pressure public officials to promote the passage of certain laws.

17. _____ works to assist a group to develop into a well functioning team by helping it to define its goals, to analyze tasks and the way tasks are performed, and to examine relationships among workers.
  * a. Team building
    b. Lobbing
    c. Task analysis
    d. Social support

18. Consultants ...
    a. are not experts
  * b. generally take a long-term approach to problem solving
    c. should have a vested interest in organization they are evaluating
    d. typically do not charge fees for their work

19. _____ are citizen groups which have come together to conquer a community social problem or to ensure that the community develops in a healthy manner.
    a. Team building groups
* b. Community development corporations
    c. Public policy makers
    d. Gatekeepers

20. John wants to join a self-help group for recovering cocaine users, but doesn't know how to find one. He should contact a(n) _____ in order to get information.
    a. consultant
    b. amicus curiae
    c. public policy center
* d. clearinghouse

21. Large enabling systems...
    a. may actually threaten the autonomy of private businesses and thus have negative effects.
    b. increase the likelihood that resources will be distributed equitably throughout the community.
    c. are useful for detecting "cracks" in the service system.
* d. All of the above are true.

22. Which of the following is NOT a disadvantage of enabling systems?
    a. conflicting goals between geographically diverse satellite organizations may lead to conflict.
* b. they discourage social support in the community.
    c. different community services may be in different stages of development.
    d. enabling systems may become overcontrolling and too parental.

23. A department store hires a psychologist to assess the best way to meet the needs of customers in wheelchairs. After this consultation, the store installs ramps at all its entrances for persons in wheelchairs. In this example, the department store is the _____ and wheelchair-bound customers are _____.
    a. consultant; clients
    b. client; consultee
* c. consultee; client
    d. client; clients

24. The American Psychological Association is recommending that psychologists do less pro bono work.
    a. True
* b. False

25. According to the chapter, the main purpose of information dissemination should be to...
    a. improve the community
    b. to promote prevention in favor of treatment
    c. empower community members to shape their destiny
* d. all of the above

26. Consultants work _____ the consultees who hire them.
* a. with
   b. for
   c. against
   d. none of the above.

27. Imagine that you are a school superintendent. You hire a consultant to help you improve the morale and job productivity of teachers in your high school. Based on Medway and Updyke's (1985) review of the literature, we know that your decision to hire a consultant probably...
   a. will not have any impact on the teachers
   b. will improve teachers' attitudes, but not their actual teaching behaviors
   c. will change teacher's teaching behaviors, but not their work attitudes.
* d. will positively change both teachers' attitudes and their behaviors.

28. Consultants...
* a. sometimes inspire fear in consultees.
   b. generally take a short-term approach to problem solving.
   c. have vested interests in the organizations they work for.
   d. all of the above are true.

30. Which of the following is NOT an example of citizen participation?
   a. voting
   b. signing a petition
   c. joining a self-help group
* d. all of the above are examples of citizen participation

31. According to Fairweather and Davidson (1986) people will resist educational campaigns because of...
   a. personality characteristics
   b. elements of the environment
   c. dogmatism
* d. All of the above.

32. In their research on pregnant teens, Seitz, Apfel, and Rosenbaum (1991)...
   a. used only one measure--failing grades--to evaluate an intervention program for pregnant teens.
   b. found that using multiple measures--including failing grades and grade point average--was unnecessary scientifically.
* c. found that pregnant teens benefitted from their intervention program on several outcome measures.
   d. did not use any outcome measures in their research.

33. Which of the following is a <u>disadvantage</u> of education and information dissemination?
   a. it is relatively expensive
   b. it reaches only a limited number of people
* c. educational efforts may go astray and have unexpected negative effects.
   d. education is not revered in the United States.

34. Which concept refers to how findings from science are made relevant to governmental and organizational policy?
      a. public policy
*   b. policy science
      c. agenda setting
      d. gate keeping

35. Which of the following statements is true?
      a. Most community psychologists prefer to ignore public policy.
      b. Most community psychologists generally believe that science and politics are separable entities.
      c. Virtually all community psychologists believe that public policy decisions on AIDS should not wait for the accumulation of scientific data.
*   d. Most community psychologists generally believe that science and politics are inseparable entities.

36. Much research on AIDS has forced citizens to think about and question the safety of their own sexual habits. To this extent, research has a(n)...
*   a. conceptual purpose
      b. instrumental purpose
      c. purposive mode
      d. predictive mode

37. After many years of research, scientific data have demonstrated the hazardous effects of second-hand smoke inhalation. Based on this research, most commercial airplane flights within the United States have outlawed cigarette smoking. In this case, scientific research played a(n)...
      a. conceptual purpose
*   b. instrumental purpose
      c. purposive mode
      d. predictive mode

38. Research designed to forecast changes in the future or whether changes will be accepted is called _____.
*   a. predictive
      b. purposive
      c. persuasive
      d. instrumental

39. Research on the hazards of second-hand cigarette smoke inhalation has caused many legislators to push for tougher anti-smoking laws. In this case, scientific research had a _____ purpose.
      a. instrumental
      b. conceptual
*   c. persuasive
      d. predictive

40. Alcoholics Anonymous is an example of a mutual assistance group.
*   a. True
      b. False

Identification of Terms

1. Personality trait of persons who believe that others, or fate, control reinforcers in the world. (Answer= Locus of control).

2. Groups consisting of lay persons whose experiences and common situations help to motivate other group members. (Answer = Self-help or mutual assistance groups).

3. Organizations which help to direct people towards appropriate self-help groups. (Answer= Clearinghouse).

4. Friend of the court. (Answer= Amicus curiae).

5. Purpose of research designed to forecast what change will occur in the future or whether changes will be accepted. (Answer= Predictive purpose).

6. Purpose of research aimed to change the way people think about social problems and solutions. (Answer= Conceptual purpose).

7. To pressure legislators to pass certain laws. (Answer= Lobby).

8. Structural gaps in service systems. (Answer= Cracks).

9. Another word for voluntary consultation. (Answer= Pro bono).

10. Adjective for persons with closed minds. (Answer= Dogmatic).

Food For Thought

I. What are the disadvantages of hiring a consultant? List at least three and give concrete examples of each one.

[Answer notes: Answers should include the expense of hiring good consultants, the fear they often instill in organizations, their time-limited work, and overly ambitious expectations from some within the organization.]

II. There has been much debate about health care reform in the United States. In particular, President Clinton tried to introduce health care reform to the American public. However, his initial plans for universal health care failed drastically. Explain why this might have happened according to Fairweather and Davidson's (1986) "two phenomena" model.

III. State the difference between the following terms: (a) Amicus curiae, (b) consultant, (c) lobbyist.

IV. If you had to choose one method to create and sustain social change on an issue that was important to you, which method would you choose? Why that one?

V. List three disadvantages to public policy change. Give concrete examples of each one.

[Answer notes: Responses should include the exclusive interest of some scientists to promote their own careers, negative public perceptions, dependency on voter turn-out, and the tedious nature of reforming the law.]

Key Terms

acculturation
amicus curiae
agenda setting
citizen participation
clearinghouse
client
community development corps
conceptual purpose of research
consultant
consultee
cracks
deinstitutionalization
dogmatic (personality)
empowerment
enabling system
external locus of control
gatekeepers
grass roots activism
information dissemination
instrumental purpose of research
internal locus of control
lobby
mutual aid
neighborhood association
networks
persuasive purpose of research
planned change
policy science
predictive purpose of research
professional change agent
public policy
self-help
self-help group
social support
team building
umbrella organization

Recommended Films

<u>Building Hope: Community Development In America</u> (60 minutes). Since the 1960's, Community Development Corporations (CDC's) have united neighborhood residents, business leaders, and governments to revitalize distressed communities. This video traces the development of the CDC movement over the past 30 years. PBS Video, 1320 Braddock Place, Alexandria, VA, 22314-1698.

<u>Making Government Work</u> (60 minutes). Explores Chicago citizen groups which have joined with government officials to preserve manufacturing jobs, revitalize parks, and prevent crime. PBS Video, 1320 Braddock Place,

Alexandria, VA, 22314-1698.

Reinventing Government In America (60 minutes). Vice President Al Gore provides insights on his effort to "reinvent" the federal government. The program highlights six communities that are trying to instill a customer-driven attitude at all levels. PBS Adult Learning Satellite Service, 1320 Braddock Place, Alexandria, VA, 22314-1698. Fax: 703-739-8495.

Visions of America: The Hoover Institution Series on Congressional Accountability and Reform (60 minutes). Explores the link between the way Congress is structured and operates and the decisions that flow from it in the form of laws and appropriations. PBS Adult Learning Satellite Service, 1320 Braddock Place, Alexandria, VA, 22314-1698. Fax: 703-739-8495.

CHAPTER 5

STRESS, COPING, AND SOCIAL SUPPORT:

TOWARD COMMUNITY MENTAL HEALTH

Introduction

This chapter introduces students to distinctions between the various models of mental health (i.e., psychoanalytic, behavioral, and humanistic). After reviewing these models and various types of mental health professionals, the chapter presents a discussion on stress and how people react to it. Various factors influencing stress reactions are discussed, including chronic versus acute stress, hassles, and social integration. Coping strategies are discussed in detail, including various types of social support, information and education, and sports and exercise. Students are presented with numerous examples from the community literature.

Lecture and Notes

I. The Medical Model: Psychoanalytic Approach

Sigmund Freud (1856-1939), one of the most influential figures in both psychology and psychiatry, developed one of the first comprehensive models of mental illness. Freud hypothesized all psychological disorders resulted from an incomplete psychosexual development during the five stages of personality development (oral, anal, phallic, latency, and genital). Disorders are manifested through defense mechanisms formed in response to the struggles among three personality structures (id, ego, and superego). Although acknowledging the role of biology in the developmental sequence, Freud advocated the use of free association and verbal therapy as the primary treatment modalities.

Subsequent theorists (Carl Gustav Jung, Alfred Adler, Karen Horney, & Erik Erikson) challenged Freud's original theoretical propositions. Criticizing his reliance on clinical experience and a restricted sample of clients, many argued for an increased emphasis on gender and culture. Furthermore, the ineffectiveness of traditional psychoanalysis with severely mentally ill persons coupled with advances in psychopharmacology fueled a schism within the psychoanalytic approach. This resulted in two separate treatment approaches: biological psychiatry (medical model) and traditional psychoanalytic individual verbal therapy.

II. The Behavioral Model: The Social-Learning Approach

Rejecting both Freud's developmental theory and the introspection method advocated by Wilhelm Wundt, J. B. Watson extended Pavlov's classical conditioning paradigm to the understanding of human behavior. Watson emphasized the importance of a scientific approach to studying the human condition and believed behavior was an important phenomena in its own right. B.F. Skinner introduced radical behaviorism based on the principles of operant conditioning. Skinner believed behavior can be best understood as a function of its consequences and introduced the concept of reinforcement.

Watson and Skinner greatly influenced subsequent theory and research. Examples include Seligman's learned helplessness model of depression and treatment techniques such as systematic desensitization for phobias.

III. The Humanistic Model

The 1960's witnessed the growth of the human rights movement and a divergence from the traditional medical model of mental illness. Increased emphasis was placed on the unique experience of the individual and the pernicious effects of diagnostic labeling. In addition, American psychologist Carl Rogers developed client-centered therapy which facilitates client self-reflection. The humanistic model incorporates both individual and group therapy sessions.

IV. Stress & Responses to Stress

Stress is a complex phenomenon which can be generally defined as "a call for action when one's capabilities are perceived as falling short of the needed personal resources." Hans Seyle did classic work on the general adaptation syndrome, which consists of three stages: alarm, resistance, exhaustion. Despite popular beliefs, the relationship between stress and illness is weak in magnitude. Variables such as hardiness, locus of control, a sense of helplessness, chronic anxiety, and low self-esteem might moderate the effects of stress, although the data are mixed.

Holmes and Rahe (1967) studies life events as a source of stress, and found that negative as well as positive life events often require psychological adjustment. Much research in this area has used an instrument called the Life Events Questionnaire. However, research by Lazarus and Folkman (1984) using the Hassles Scale indicates that exposure to numerous daily hassles can also lead to health problems. Finally, chronic stress is more strongly associated with depressive symptoms than acute stress.

The physical environment can also introduce stress and contribute to physical illness. The chapter gives several examples, including research by Paulus et al. (1978), who found higher blood pressure rates in prisoners living in overcrowded quarters. Also, Bronzaft (1981) demonstrated that students living on the nosy side of a school performed less well than those living on the crowded side.

Social integration can promote better mental health within communities. One interesting study by Holahan et al. (1983) found more psychological symptoms among Blacks than Whites. However, Blacks were less socially integrated into their communities than Whites. Also, Blacks low in social integration showed more symptoms than either Blacks or Whites high in social integration. Thus, personal involvement with community institutions is an important component of mental health.

V. Coping Strategies.

Social Support

Social support is a concept that was introduced by Cassell (1974) and expanded by Caplan (1974). The literature on social support is currently booming. Social support is commonly provided in "mutual help groups," which include organizations such as Alcoholics Anonymous and Overeaters Anonymous. Ironically, researchers don't quite know the mechanism by which social support works. There are three proposed mechanisms:

a) Social embeddedness--refers to the number of connections a person has to significant others who might be able to offer support.

b) Enacted support--refers to availability of actual support. Specifically, this refers to the number of friends who can actually provide support.

c) Perceived social support--refers to the cognitive appraisal of being reliably connected to others. In other words, it may be the <u>perceived</u> rather than the <u>actual</u> interpersonal support which is most helpful. This concept has received the most empirical investigation.

Support groups exist for all types of problems including cancer patients, the bereaved, rape victims, chronic stress, suicide attempters, adolescent mothers, scoliosis patients, handicapped children, and the homeless...just to name a few.

Social support may be effective through one of three routes:

a) the direct effects of social support--means that interpersonal contact directly promotes healthier behaviors (e.g., sticking to a diet).

b) the indirect effects of social support--means that interpersonal contact promotes healthier behaviors and well-being by reducing the perceived severity of a stressor.

c) interactive effects (buffering effects)--means that interpersonal contact helps to improve the adverse effects of stressful events by increasing the recognition, quality, and quantity of coping resources. In addition, teaching coping skills may actually promote healthier behaviors and enhance life, a phenomenon called a <u>boostering effect</u>.

Research has not identified one method which best explains all the data. For example, social support offered direct relief to an inner-city elderly population, although no buffering effects were observed. However, buffering effects were reported among college students who received social support while waiting to answer personal questions on videotape.

Social support is a two-way exchange process. It is reciprocal, a phenomenon called <u>the transactional nature of social support</u>. Unfortunately, it is very hard to measure the process of social support. Three popular scales are:

(a) <u>Inventory of Socially Supportive Behaviors</u>
    (Barrera et al., 1981)

(b) <u>The Social Support Behaviors Scale</u>
    (Vaux, Riedel, & Stewart, 1987)

(c) <u>Social Support Questionnaire</u> (Sarason, 1983).

The specific social supporter can also influence the process of social support. For example, cancer patients found advice from health care providers to be helpful, but not as helpful when the same advice came from friends and family (Dunkel-Schetter, 1984). Compared to other professionals, lawyers tend to do more talking and provide more information (Toro, 1986). At the same time, the others' perceptions of the recipient influences the process of social support. Individuals are less likely to receive support if they are perceived as being responsible for, or the cause of, their problem. Similarly, we are more likely to help those who are similar to us or those whom we like.

The situation can also impede social support. For example, research on the <u>bystander effect</u> has demonstrated that as the number of potential helpers increases, each person is less likely to step forward and offer assistance. This is partially due to <u>responsibility diffusion</u>, in which we feel less responsible for another's fate when others present could also accept responsibility for helping.

A large scale Canadian survey (Gottlieb & Peters, 1991) found that the typical mutual help group participant was a middle class woman between the ages of 25 to 44. The ratio of male to female participants was 4 to 6.

The advantages of support groups and social support include:
(a) Enhanced well-being of support recipients.
(b) Enhanced sense of belonging on the part of the provider.
(c) Enhanced sense of self-esteem and self-identity on the part of the provider.
(d) Reduction of stress. People learn to reappraise the severity of their situations. Also, people learn techniques for dealing with stress.

The disadvantages of social support include:
(a) Not everybody wants to get involved or be supportive.
(b) Support can sometimes be harmful. Specifically, support can threaten a recipient's self-esteem, especially if it implies an inferior role on part of the recipient.
(c) There is often a <u>norm of reciprocity</u>, which states that we expect others to pay us back for our aid and support. However, recipients may be unable to reciprocate.
(d) Untimely support.

Information and Education

Cowen (1980) argues that mental health education should teach people how to think and make reasonable choices for themselves. Other community psychologists agree. Ketterer (1981) proposed two types of mental health education: one designed to improve coping skills and competencies and the second to promote public information strategies. Three techniques are recommended to reach these goals:

* mass media
* lectures and/or disseminations
* small group discussions

The authors provide several examples of research which examine the efficacy of mental health education.

Sports, Recreation, and Exercise

There is evidence that exercise and physical fitness help buffer the unhealthy effects of stress. Unfortunately, many people who begin exercise regiments often discontinue them. Bloom (1988) found that as many as half of the people who start an exercise program drop out within the first few months. The attrition rate increases one year later. According to Danish (1983), people discontinue exercise when it feels like an obligation and loses its intrinsically motivating characteristics.

Multiple Choice Questions

1. _____ is associated with the belief that people have certain inalienable rights and should be treated with dignity.
   * a. Humanism
   b. Community psychiatry
   c. Forensic psychology
   d. Social learning theory

2. Stress responses include which of the following?
   a. high blood pressure
   b. ulcers
   c. learned helplessness
   * d. all of the above

3. Which of the following represents the correct order of stages in the general adaptation syndrome?
   a. alarm; exhaustion; resistance
   b. exhaustion; alarm; resistance
   * c. alarm; resistance; exhaustion
   d. resistance; alarm; exhaustion

4. Studies on the relationship between stress and physical illness ...
   a. are usually very well designed.
   b. show a strong positive relationship between stress and illness.
   c. show correlations ranging between .4 and .6 between stress and illness.
   * d. show a weak but positive relationship between stress and illness.

5. Immunoglobin...
   a. generally increases during times of stress.
   * b. protects people from illness.
   c. causes people to become stressed.
   d. both a & c are true.

6. _____ is typified by a sense of personal control, a sense of commitment to work and self, and a tendency to perceive change as a challenge rather than a threat.
   * a. Hardiness
   b. Self-esteem
   c. Chronic anxiety
   d. None of the above

7. According to Holmes and Rahe (1967), subjects rated _____ as the most stressful life event.
   a. divorce
   b. marital separation
   * c. death of a spouse
   d. being fired from a job

8. According to research by Holmes and Rahe (1967), the three most stressful life events are _____ (#1), _____ (#2), and _____ (#3).
   a. death of a spouse; personal injury or illness; divorce
   b. divorce; death of a spouse; personal injury or illness
   c. being fired; divorce; personal injury or illness
   * d. death of a spouse; divorce; marital separation

9. Life changes are most stressful when they are ...
   * a. unpredictable or uncontrollable
   b. unpredictable or loud
   c. uncontrollable or loud
   d. none of the above

10. Horowitz and colleagues (1977) developed a questionnaire called...
    a. the Hassles Scale
    * b. the Life Events Questionnaire
    c. the Chronic Stress Inventory
    d. the Stress Survey

11. Research by Lazarus and Folkman has shown that exposure to a single life stressor is worse than the exposure to numerous daily annoyances.
    a. True
    * b. False

12. McGonagle and Kessler (1990) found that depressive symptoms were more strongly related to _____ than _____.
    a. daily hassles; chronic stress
    b. chronic stress; daily hassles
    * c. chronic stress; acute stress
    d. acute stress; daily hassles

13. Children living in flight paths of the Los Angeles airport displayed _____ than children not living near the airport.
    a. higher blood pressure
    b. lower math scores
    c. less persistent problem-solving skills
    * d. all of the above

14. Adams (1992) examined the effects of urban versus suburban living conditions on psychological health. The authors found...
    * a. no differences between urban and suburban residents in satisfaction with neighborhood.
    b. suburban residents expressed greater dissatisfaction with their neighborhoods than urban residents.
    c. urban residents expressed greater dissatisfaction with their neighborhoods than suburban residents.
    d. social support was important for individuals living in urban but not suburban settings.

15. Holahan et al. (1983) found that Blacks reported significantly fewer psychological symptoms than Whites.
    a. True
    * b. False

16. Research by Aldwin and Greenberger (1987) has shown that depression is related to _____ in Korean youths and _____ in Caucasian youths.
    a. academic stress; parental depression
    * b. parental traditionalism; academic stress
    c. parental traditionalism; parental depression
    d. parental depression; academic work

17. Aldwin and Greenberger (1987) found that Korean youths overall were more depressed than Caucasian youths.
    * a. True
    b. False

18. Self-help groups ...
    * a. are also called mutual-help groups.
    b. must be led by professionals.
    c. cannot be used to help individual with severe problems such as alcoholism or gambling.
    d. all of the above are true.

19. _____ can be defined as an exchange of resources between two individuals perceived by the provider or the recipient to be intended to enhance the well-being of the recipient.
    a. Mental health education
    * b. social support
    c. stress
    d. Social integration

20. Which of the following terms is not related to the more general concept of social support?
    a. social embeddedness
    b. enacted support
    * c. social constructivism
    d. perceived social support

21. _____ refers to the cognitive appraisal of being reliably connected to others.
    a. Social embeddedness
    b. Enacted support
    c. The norm of reciprocity
    * d. Perceived social support

22. _____ is the number of connections that an individuals has to significant others.
    a. Enacted support
    b. Social support
  * c. Social embeddedness
    d. Perceived social support

23. _____ refers to the availability of actual support.
  * a. Enacted support
    b. Social support
    c. Social embeddedness
    d. Perceived social support

24. Your friend teaches you coping skills so that you can work through your divorce with minimal emotional distress. This is an example of ...
    a. the direct effects of social support.
    b. the indirect effects of social support.
  * c. the buffering effects of social support.
    d. the boostering effects of social support.

25. In order to assist you in working on a math problem, your brother shows you how to break down the problem into smaller sections. This is an example of ...
    a. the direct effects of social support.
  * b. the indirect effects of social support.
    c. the buffering effects of social support.
    d. the boostering effects of social support.

26. In order to help you manage to cope with your growing medical expenses, your father lends you five hundred dollars. This is an example of ...
  * a. the direct effects of social support.
    b. the indirect effects of social support.
    c. the buffering effects of social support.
    d. the boostering effects of social support.

27. Your therapist convinces you that you are mentally healthy by showing you all of your wonderful life accomplishments. This is an example of...
    a. the direct effects of social support.
    b. the indirect effects of social support.
    c. the buffering effects of social support.
  * d. the boostering effects of social support.

28. Social support works because it is a two-way phenomenon in which one persons helps another, and visa-versa. This reflects the ...
    a. indirect effects of social support.
    b. the interactive effects of social support.
  * c. the transactional nature of social support.
    d. the boostering effects of social support.

29. Which of the following is not a social support inventory listed in the chapter?
   * a. the Coping With Hassles Questionnaire
   b. the Inventory of Socially Supportive Behaviors
   c. the Social Support Behaviors Scale
   d. the Social Support Questionnaire

30. _____ is the phenomenon in which we feel less responsible for another's fate when others present could also accept responsibility.
   a. The bystander effect
   * b. Responsibility diffusion
   c. The norm of reciprocity
   d. Perceived social support

31. Gottlieb and Peters (1991) conducted a large-scale survey of Canadians who attend mutual-help groups. The authors found that the typical participant is ...
   a. a middle class male between 25 and 44 years old.
   b. an lower class female between 25 and 44 years old.
   * c. a middle class female between 25 and 44 years old.
   d. a upper class female between 35 and 45 year old.

32. The traditional psychoanalytic approach to the treatment of mental illness includes
   a. biological interventions
   * b. individual verbal therapy
   c. community residences
   d. hospitalization

33. According to Freud, all psychological disorders are the result of incomplete_____
   a. defense mechanisms.
   b. classical conditioning.
   c. collective unconscious.
   * d. psychosexual development.

34. Freud was often criticized for ignoring the impact of _____ and _____ on personality development.
   a. biology; parents
   b. gender; biology
   c. society; biology
   * d. gender; culture

35. The mental illness model based on biological explanations for mental disorders is...
   a. the behavioral Model
   b. the humanistic Model
   * c. the medical Model
   d. the psychiatric Model

36. The _____ rejects the psychoanalytic approach and introspection method for the understanding of mental health.
   a. the medical model
 * b. the behavioral model
   c. the humanistic model
   d. the biological model

37. _____ refers to the principle that behavior is more likely to occur when it is reinforced or rewarded.
   a. Classical conditioning
   b. A conditioned response
 * c. Operant conditioning
   d. Desensitization

38. The principles of social learning theory have been extended to explain depression as a form of.....
   a. defense mechanisms.
   b. extended introspection.
   c. an unconditioned stimulus.
 * d. learned helplessness.

39. The mental illness model closely associated with the growth of the human rights movement was....
   a. the behavioral model
 * b. the humanistic model
   c. the medical model
   d. the Renaissance model

40. The humanistic model emphasizes the use of _____ in the treatment of mental disorders.
   a. individual verbal therapy
   b. group verbal therapy
   c. medicine
 * d. both a & b

41. Shinn et al.'s (1984) research on bereavement found that _____ was valuable in the early stages of grieving, while _____ was important in the later stages.
   a. perceived social support; enacted social support
   b. support for reintegration; empathy
 * c. emotional support; support for reintegration
   d. perceived social support; enacted support

42. According to Cowen (1980), the goal of mental health education is to teach people _____ to think.
 * a. how
   b. what
   c. when
   d. all of the above

43. According to Ketterer (1981), mental health educators use three techniques to promote mental health. Which of the following is NOT one of the techniques?
* a. exercise
  b. mass media
  c. lectures and/or demonstrations
  d. small group discussions

44. Munoz et al. (1982) broadcasted a series of television segments about depression, self-control, and social learning. Their intervention resulted in observers ...
  a. stopping thoughts about upsetting events.
  b. taking more time to relax
  c. reporting less depression--especially among those who initially scored very high on depression measures.
* d. all of the above

45. According to Danish (1983), adherence to physical exercise decreases when...
  a. exercise feels like an obligation.
  b. exercise is intrinsically motivated.
* c. exercise is no longer intrinsically motivated.
  d. there are no longer external rewards for exercising.

Identification of Terms

1. Therapy in which the role of the therapist is to facilitate the client's reflection upon his or her experiences (Answer= Client-centered therapy).

2. A call for action when one's capabilities are perceived as falling short of the needed personal resources. (Answer= Stress).

3. Third stage of the general adaptation syndrome. (Answer= Exhaustion).

4. Trait characterized by a sense of personal control, a sense of commitment to work and self, and a tendency to perceive change as a challenge rather than as a threat. (Answer= Hardiness).

5. Term for self-inspection introduced by Wilhelm Wundt. (Answer= Introspection).

6. The number of connections that an individual has to significant others who might offer assistance. (Answer= Social embeddedness).

7. The cognitive appraisal of being reliably connected to others. (Answer= Perceived social support).

8. Our expectation to reciprocate for those who have helped us out. (Answer= Norm of reciprocity).

9. Effects of social support which enhances positive life events. (Answer= Boostering effects).

10. The training model for clinical psychologists. (Answer= Scientist-practitioner model).

Food For Thought

I. Imagine that you are the director of a mental health center who is preparing a marketing presentation. First, you explain that one of your responsibilities is to inform clients about the different services provided at the center. Because you run a very comprehensive program, you are proud of the fact that all mental health models are represented. For your presentation, what three primary mental health/illness models would you discuss? What are the differences between each model? What type of treatment would your clients expect to receive from each?

[Answer notes: Discuss the medical, humanistic, and behavioral models, and their prospective philosophical differences. Student's should demonstrate some understanding of treatment based upon medical intervention, learning theory principles, and client centered therapy.]

II. Imagine that you are getting divorced and feel very stressed and depressed. The divorce is very costly, some family members are angry with you, and you now have to find a new place to live. Give examples of how your friends could provide you with (a) direct effects of social support, (b) indirect effects of social support, (c) buffering effects of social support, and (d) boostering effects of social support. Be specific.

[Answer notes: Students should demonstrate a distinct understanding of these different effects of social support and provide concrete examples of each.]

III. Research by Lazarus and Folkman (1984) has demonstrated that numerous hassles can contribute to poorer health. What are the minor hassles that <u>you</u> experience that interfere with you psychological well-being? List your top seven daily hassles? How do you think you could get rid of them?

IV. You tell your parents that your college dormitory is making you sick because the rooms are so small and noisy. Your parents tell you to stop complaining and that the problem "is all in your head." Do you agree or disagree with your parents? Is it true that the physical environment cannot impair your health in this way? Cite date to justify your answer.

[Answer notes: Answer should integrate research by Paulus et al. (1978), Wener & Keys (1988), Cohen et al. (1986), and Bronzaft (1981) to demonstrate the effects of environmental conditions on health and behavior.]

V. Many people believe that there are no disadvantages to having social support. Why is this belief false? What are the drawbacks to social support? Give examples.

[Answer notes: Threats to self-esteem, norm of reciprocity, and poor timing should be discussed].

Key Terms

Acute stress
Alarm stage

Behavioral model
Boostering effects of social support
Bystander effect
Buffering effects of social support
Certified alcohol counselors
Chronic stress
Classical conditioning
Client-centered therapy
Clinical psychologists
Conditioned response
Conditioned stimulus
Desensitization
Diagnostic and Statistical Manual
Direct effects of social support
Enacted support
Exhaustion stage
General adaptation syndrome (GAS)
Hardiness
Hassles Scale
Humanistic model
Indirect effects of social support
Interactive effects of social support
International Code of Diagnosis
Introspection
Labeling
Learned helplessness
Life Events Questionnaire
Medical model
Mental health education
Moderating factors
Mutual help groups
Norm of reciprocity
Operant conditioning
Perceived social support
Psychiatric nurses
Psychiatric rehabilitation counselors
Psychiatrists
Reinforced (response)
Resistance stage
Responsibility diffusion
Scientist-practitioner model
Self-help groups
Social embeddedness
Social integration
Social support
Social workers
Stress
Therapist
Transactional nature of social support
Unconditioned response
Unconditioned stimulus
Vocational counselors

Recommended Films

<u>Can't Slow Down</u> (28 minutes). This program examines Americans' increasingly hurried and pressured life style and it's effects on our health and relationships. Films For The Humanities Inc., P.O. Box 2053, Princeton, New Jersey, 08543-2053.

<u>Health, Mind, and Behavior</u> (60 minutes). Examines the relationship between the mind and body while emphasizing the bio-psycho-social model. The Annenberg/CPB Project, 901 E. Street, NW, Washington, DC 20004-2037. Fax: 802-864-9846.

<u>The Clinical Psychologist</u> (24 minutes). Profiling the work of a typical therapist, this video follows a clinical psychologist as he counsels a client and the client's family. Insight Media Inc., 2162 Broadway, New York, New York, 10024.

<u>The Caring Helper</u> (30 minutes). Teaches how to enhance self-esteem while promoting self-disclosure, especially for persons in distress. Insight Media Inc., 2162 Broadway, New York, New York, 10024.

<u>Emotion and Illness</u> (30 minutes). This program visits classes for people under stress, hospital cancer wards, and a support group for breast cancer patients to show how emotions are being treated in order to improve health. Films For The Humanities Inc., P.O. Box 2053, Princeton, New Jersey, 08543-2053.

<u>Our Nation Under Stress</u> (52 minutes). This program explains what causes stress, its consequences, and demonstrates how stress can be turned into a positive force. Films For The Humanities Inc., P.O. Box 2053, Princeton, New Jersey, 08543-2053.

<u>Reducing Stress</u> (19 minutes). This program explains that a wide variety of physical problems, including heart attacks and stroke, can be caused by stress. Physical and mental relaxation techniques are presented, as well as recommended life changes. Films For The Humanities Inc., P.O. Box 2053, Princeton, New Jersey, 08543-2053.

<u>Stress</u> (26 minutes). This program looks at the many ways stress can affect people of all ages and demonstrates proven methods of coping with the pressures of life. Films For The Humanities Inc., P.O. Box 2053, Princeton, New Jersey, 08543-2053.

<u>The Nature of Stress</u> (60 minutes). This program examines the long-term effects of stress and how to reduce them. Examples come from the unemployed, the overworked, and Vietnam veterans. The Annenberg/CPB Project, 901 E. Street, NW, Washington, DC 20004-2037. Fax: 802-864-9846.

<u>Women And Stress</u> (28 minutes). This special episode of the Phil Donahue program discusses how women experience stress the same as men but tend to conceal their reactions. Films For The Humanities Inc., P.O. Box 2053, Princeton, New Jersey, 08543-2053.

CHAPTER 6

THE SERIOUSLY MENTALLY DISORDERED:

BACK TO THE COMMUNITY

Introduction

An historical account of mental health/illness conceptualization and treatment demonstrates the inextricable influence of socio-political agendas. The present chapter outlines the historical differences in mental health conceptualization and subsequent treatments. Students are presented with an overview of the "deinstitutionalization" movement and related issues from a community psychological prospective.

Lectures and Notes

I. Historical Notes About Mental Disorder

The emphasis placed on the study of mental health/illness has varied across cultures and within cultures across time.
Early theorizing and advancement were recorded in both the ancient Chinese and Greek cultures. For example, Chinese historical texts and folklore document early medical advancements including the use of acupuncture as an anesthetic (Wah Torr "the Father of Chinese medicine") and the first classification system of herbs used in medicine (Sun Lone Tse) dating back to 600 -700 B.C. Furthermore, to most Chinese (ancient and modern) physical and psychological well-being is thought to depend on a balance between two natural forces Yin (female force) and Yan (male force).

Hippocrates (circa 460-377 B.C.) known as "the Father of Western Medicine" proposed an individual's mental health is governed by four humors. Specifically, differential mood states were thought to be caused by individual fluctuations in levels of blood, phlegm, yellow bile, and black bile.

Following the collapse of the Roman Empire in Europe (circa 500 A.D.) the predominant view of mental illness was based on a supernatural or religious etiological perspective. Mentally disordered people were viewed as "sinners" or of deviant moral character and often the recipients of government or church sanctioned persecution. This view predominated western societies for approximately 900 years and coincided with what has become to be known as the "dark ages".

During the Renaissance period (1400 - 1700) a humanistic philosophy began to develop. Thus, mentally disordered individual's began to gain indirect benefits from the belief that all people had certain inalienable rights and should be treated with dignity. It was also during this period (mid 1600's) that the containment of the mentally disordered in asylums was established. The Unites States followed with the establishment of the first asylum in the late 1700's.

During the 1800's numerous philosophical and scientific developments continued to reform the mental health movement. Benjamin Rush ("the Father of American Psychiatry") wrote the first treatise on psychiatry and established its first academic course. Dorothea Dix lobbied for the building of mental health hospitals, and early nomenclatures (classifications) of mental illness were being developed. Furthermore, the increased recognition of Louis Pasteur's germ theory mediated the disease conceptualization of mental illness. This period also marked the separate development of both the American Psychological and American Psychiatric Associations.

From 1875 - 1940 the government assumed primary responsibility for the care of the mentally disordered. Approximately two-thirds of the psychiatric population resided in state-run hospitals; however, more often than not, patients received little treatment. Meanwhile, the development of private psychiatric hospitals facilitated the development of community psychiatry based on the philosophy that treatment should be conducted with the least restrictive method in the least restrictive environment.

The beginning of the 1960's marked the development of further mental health care reform. The introduction of psychotropic drugs concomitant with the philosophy of community psychiatry precipitated the development of outpatient treatment facilities and community residences. Furthermore, patient rights became a primary concern reflected in the development of organizations such as the National Alliance for the Mentally Ill.

Presently, mental health reform must include systematic planning. In the past decade urban cities have witnessed an increasing number of homeless mentally disordered and concomitant decrease in financial support.

II. Deinstitutionalization

Deinstitutionalization has come to stand for a complex interaction among ideological and practical concerns regarding present mental health care reform. Perspectives of deinstitutionalization have included John Talbott's terming it _transinstitutionalization_ describing the transferring of patients to multiple substandard treatment facilities.

Popular conceptions of deinstitutionalization have ranged from negative to positive. Positive perceptions include the view that patients are moved from enormous remote hospitals to community residences. However, negative perceptions have included the equating of deinstitutionalization with homelessness or the placing of individuals into the community with little support services.

In an attempt to reconcile many of the conflicting views of deinstitutionalization, some mental health care experts have proposed the term should be used as a "semantic mechanism" to capture the complex and often contradictory issues related to mental health care reform. Thus, the term can carry many explicit and implicit meanings.

It has been argued that an important impetus for deinstitutionalization was that of budgetary constraints. This has resulted in conflicting views concerning mental health reform based solely on practical concerns.

Bachrach (1989) provided a more heuristic definition of deinstitutionalization consistent with the view that mental health care reform should plan for long-term mental health consequences. His definition assumes three primary processes involved in mental health care reform:

* <u>depopulation</u> - the reduction of state hospital censuses.
* <u>diversion</u> - the deflection of potential institutional admissions to community-based service settings.
* <u>decentralization</u> - the broadening of responsibility for patient care to multiple entities.

Furthermore, mental health care reform should be based on three elements: facts, process, and philosophy.

<u>The Many Aspects of Deinstitutionalization</u>

Although complex, the issues surrounding deinstitutionalization may be best conceptualized from philosophical, biomedical, economic, sociological, and psychological perspectives. It has been proposed that the first three perspectives may better account for the reasons behind its occurrence. Moreover, sociological and psychological factors may explain the less than optimal effect of enhancing the quality of life for the mentally disordered.

a. <u>philosophical</u>- during the 1960's "humanism" appeared to reach its peak. This was exemplified in the growth of programs developed to assist the less fortunate such as the Peace Corp and Head Start.

b. <u>biomedical</u>- the development and refinement of psychotropic medication facilitated the treatment of once "unmanageable" disorders. Thus, professionals were better able to treat the mentally disordered using the least restrictive method.

c. <u>economic</u>- argued by some mental health care experts to be the primary impetus for deinstitutionalization. For example, Warner (1989) has reported an association between labor demand and the development of rehabilitative programs. Further evidence suggests the number of state psychiatric hospital admittances was related to the qualitative state of the economy. Thus, the better the economy the fewer state psychiatric hospital admittances.

d. <u>sociological</u>- perspectives of the "less than optimal" effect of deinstitutionalization, have focused on, among others, issues of adequate housing, public relations, adequate discharge planning, and support systems. Resistance among community members regarding the building of half way houses, inadequate social and daily living skills among those discharged, and the increasing use of ill prepared facilities such as board-and-care-homes and nursing homes, have contributed to the lamentable conditions of the mentally disordered.

"Deinstitutionalization" has also been viewed as a reason for the increasing number of mental health patients in the criminal justice system. Studies tracking chronic mentally disordered patients have demonstrated criminal justice services to be the most frequently used. This has been attributed to the inability or unwillingness of those released from hospitals to follow through on their own aftercare. Furthermore, the legal system's perspective of mental illness may diminish the likelihood of those incarcerated receiving mental health treatment.

e. <u>psychological</u> - perspectives of the factors hindering the progress of "deinstitutionalization" have included the effects of stigmatization and victimization. It has been found that certain demographic groups (i.e., homeless females) have a greater probability of being prone to victimization. Furthermore, "stereotypes" about the mentally disordered may further impede the reintegration process associated with "deinstitutionalization".

Common Alternatives To Deinstitutionalization

An ideal setting for the institutionalized individual would be one which enhances his or her well-being due to an optimal fit between the individual's competencies and the support provided in the environment. However, this often is not the case with community placements primarily based upon economic concerns rather than individual competencies. An overview of the various forms of care for the mentally disordered reveals marginal changes since the days of institutionalization. Research indicates the following facilities care for the chronic mentally disordered:

* <u>nursing homes</u> - it is estimated that 1.15 million mentally disordered reside in nursing homes. The nursing home industry is the largest system of long-term care for the severely and persistently mentally disordered.
* <u>board-and-care homes</u> - it is estimated that 400,000 chronically mentally disordered reside in these settings. They consist of community-based shelter-care facilities including group homes and family care homes. This industry is relatively unregulated and more decentralized than nursing homes.
* <u>mental hospitals</u> - account for approximately 250,000 of chronically mentally disordered.
* <u>family settings</u> - account for approximately 150,000 to 170,000 of the chronically mentally disordered.
* <u>jails and homelessness</u> - account for the remaining percentage of the chronically mentally disordered.

The present fragmentation of care for the mentally disordered reflects a shift from a mental health care system to a predominantly welfare system.

Measuring "Success" of Deinstitutionalized Persons

Assessing the effectiveness of deinstitutionalization has proven to be a complex task. In part, this complexity has been attributed to the varying criteria employed for demarcating a successful outcome. The typical measures employed have been social integration and recidivism. However, these measures have proven to be fairly narrow in their scope. An overview of other psychological fields has also demonstrated varying criteria for success. Residents, staff, and family members of community care facilities often express quality of life as an outcome measure. Federal officials and academics cite psychosocial functioning. Moreover, clinicians have demonstrated different criteria for different groups. Specifically, patient's ethnicity, personal characteristics, and the clinicians' perceptions of disorder severity have proved to bias the judgements of outcome ratings.

Environmental factors have also been deemed important in the success of deinstitutionalization. Research has demonstrated that individuals residing in large cities (i.e. greater than 100,000) are more likely to be precluded from involvement in community life and accessing resources. This in part appears to be attributed to the problems of travel distance and safety associated with large cities. Furthermore, the depersonalization of services and community attitudes to the mentally disordered are environmental factors associated with the success of integration into the community.

III. Beyond Deinstitutionalization

With the introduction of the Community Mental Health Act in the 1960's it was thought that a signficant reduction in the census of state hospitals could be facilitated with psychiatric treatment provided in the community. However, it appears that a lack of systematic planning and poor coordination hindered the full realization of this goal. Furthermore, it was evident that the quality of services provided was dependent upon a more comprehensive understanding of the mentally ill population.

A First Step: Epidemiological Catchment Area Study

It was hoped the introduction of the Community Mental Health Act would reduce state psychiatric hospitalizations and facilitate mental health care in the community. However, failure to realize these goals has been attributed to the lack of systematic planning, poor coordination, or the poor quality of services.

It has been argued that the quality of service depends on our knowledge of mental illness. Thus, studies have been conducted to ascertain the characteristics of the mentally disordered. In the early 1980's the NIMH surveyed the psychiatric status of more than 20,000 people in five cities. The findings of the Epidemiological Catchment Area Study suggested a 10% prevalence rate of mental illness in American Adults. These findings were consistent with the results of the Midtown Manhattan Study conducted from 1952 to 1960.

Some mental health experts argue that because of cultural norms ethnic minorities may be under-represented in epidemiological studies. For example, it has been found that Asian- and Hispanic-Americans tend to under utilize mental health services. Furthermore, when using mental health care services, ethnic minorities tend to have higher attrition rates. However, this trend is attenuated when health care providers are of similar ethnic background.

Model Programs For The Mentally Disordered Individuals

Over the years it appears that community psychologists know more about what does not work that what does. However, by evaluating pioneer programs and epidemiological investigations some innovative psychosocial rehabilitation models have been developed. The author's outline several models commonly employed today. They include:
* Lodge Societies - which encompass highly structured halfway houses or group homes which emphasize skill building and shared responsibilities.

* <u>Case management</u> - which is intensive case support including instruction in daily living skills and close monitoring and brokering of delivery of a variety of services.
* <u>Assertive community treatment (ACT)</u> - a case management program also known as mobile treatment teams which focus on the teaching of practical living skills and provide a case manager which oversees the attention to medication, service planning, and the coordination of assessment and evaluation services.

<u>The Battle Continues: Where Do We Go From Here?</u>

What have we learned since "deinstitutionalization"? It appears that mental health experts have gleaned more knowledge of what does not work then what does. However, based on the previous studies some psychosocial rehabilitation models have been developed.

Common to all of the rehabilitation models is the use of case management or intensive social support. Compared to more traditional treatments, case management;
* is more labor intensive.
* reduces both hospital use and cost.
* demonstrates variable efficacy in the reduction of symptoms and improvement of social relations.
* case managers can work with the client in residential and outpatient treatment programs which should mitigate against recidivism or relapse.
* is consistent with community psychology's empowerment philosophy.

Since "deinstitutionalization" the public has become more aware of mental health/illness. Groups such as the, National Alliance for the Mentally Ill (NAMI) have functioned both as self-help groups and political lobbying bodies.

Currently, mental health care reform is at a critical juncture. It has become increasingly important to address mental health care issues in conjunction with other health agendas. Furthermore, with the proposed national managed care or control care system it is important to acknowledge the complexity of health care reform and not fall prey to the overly optimistic view of the 1960's.

<u>Multiple Choice Questions</u>

1. "Deinstitutionalization" is best viewed as a simple phenomenon characterized by the sending of patients back into the community?
   a. True * b. False

2. "Deinstitutionalization" has been referred to as?
   a. homelessness
   b. transinstitutionalization
   c. the cutting of mental health budgets
   d. a complex set of issues relating to mental health care reform
 * e. all the above

3. _____ refers to the belief that mental health care reform had been characterized by the transferring of care from one institution to many inadequate ones.
    a. Deinstitutionalization
* b. Transinstitutionalization
    c. Managed care
    d. Case management

4. Viewed as a semantic mechanism, "deinstitutionalization" consists of concrete or _____ and implied or _____ meanings.
* a. explicit; implicit
    b. implicit; explicit
    c. singular; multiple
    d. none of the above

5. _____ refers to the shrinking of state hospital censuses through the release, transfer, or death of patients.
    a. Deflection
    b. Decentralization
    c. "Deinstitutionalization"
* d. Depopulation
    c. both b and c

6. The broadening of responsibility for patient care to multiple and diverse services is known as _____.
    a. deflection
    b. depopulation
    c. managed care
* d. decentralization

7. According to Bachrach (1989), sound mental health care policy must be based on creditable research and evidence or _____.
    a. diversion
    b. transinstitutionalization
* c. the facts
    d. ideology

8. The deflection of potential hospital admissions to community-based service settings is known as _____.
    a. deflection
    b. depopulation
    c. decentralization
* d. diversion

9. When planning for long-term mental health goals, we must know the _____, or the characteristics of the mentally disordered and the methods by which they obtain their services.
    a. philosophy
    b. case management
* c. process
    d. facts

10. _____ and historical events often determine the direction of mental health care movements and reform.
   * a. Philosophy
   b. The facts
   c. Humanism
   d. Practical concerns

11. The "deinstitutionalization" movement can be understood from a _____ perspective.
   a. biomedical
   b. economic
   c. psychological
   d. philosophical
   * e. all of the above

12. The philosophical movement most closely associated with "deinstitutionalization" during the 1960's is known as _____.
   a. empowerment
   * b. humanism
   c. Managed care
   d. Community Mental Health Care Act

13. The _____ perspective(s) of mental health care reform attributes "deinstitutionalization" to the demand for labor.
   a. humanistic
   b. sociological
   c. biomedical
   * d. economical
   e. both b and d

14. Medical advancements allowed for the treatment of once unmanageable patients using the _____ method.
   a. managed care
   b. community-based
   * c. least restrictive
   d. humanistic

15. According to Kieran et al. (1989), when the economy was good, _____ people were admitted to psychiatric hospitals.
   a. more
   b. the same amount of
   * c. fewer
   d. no relationship was found

16. Community psychologists and mental health care experts have argued that both sociological and psychological factors may have contributed to the _____ effects of "deinstitutionalization".
   a. positive
   b. optimal
   * c. less than optimal
   d. transinstitutionalization

17. Sociological factors cited as being important for the meeting of "deinstitutionalization" goals are:
- a. adequate housing
- b. public relations
- c. support systems
- * d. all of the above
- e. both a and c

18. "Deinstitutionalization" has been cited as being a major reason for the increasing number of mental health patients involved in the _____ system.
- a. managed care
- b. psychiatric hospital care
- * c. prison
- d. both a and c
- e. community care

19. Although ill prepared to provide mental health services, _____ have accounted for the care of a majority of psychiatric hospital discharges.
- a. community centers
- b. nursing homes
- c. board-and-care homes
- d. drug treatment centers
- * e. both b and c

20. Diamond and Schnee (1990), found that a majority of the services used by a group of men tracked over a period of time were provided by the _____.
- * a. criminal justice system
- b. mental health care system
- c. social service agencies
- d. both a and b

21. Because both the legal and mental health systems view mental illness similarly, the provision of care is the same from both agencies.
   a. True   * b. False

22. Psychological factors suggested to be predictive of the mental health of patients and the success of "deinstitutionalization" include:
- a. victimization
- b. adequate housing
- c. stigmatization
- d. all of the above
- * e. both a and c

23. The goal of the _____ was to "reduce the census of state hospitals and to provide treatment to maintain psychiatric patients in the community".
- a. "deinstitutionalization"
- b. managed care
- * c. Community Mental Health Act
- d. transinstitutionalization

24. The reasons given to explain the existing "patchwork" of mental health care services include_____.
   a. lack of systematic planning
   b. poor quality of services
   c. poor coordination
   d. all of the above
 * e. both b and c

25. Studies investigating the prevalence of mental illness in the general population have suggested approximately _____ American Adults have some form of mental illness.
   a. 2 of 10
 * b. 1 of 10
   c. 5 of 10
   d. 4 of 10

26. According to Sue et al. (1991), ethnic minorities are_____ likely to terminate treatments when the mental health care providers are of similar ethnic background.
 * a. less
   b. more
   c. no relationship was found

27. Common to many of the new psychosocial rehabilitation models is the use of_____ and training in daily living skills.
   a. empowerment
   b. outpatient care
 * c. case management
   d. medication

28. Research indicates that case management has had an effect on _____. However, strong support has not been found for its effects on _____.
   a. recidivism; hospital costs
   b. empowerment; outpatient treatment
 * c. hospital use and costs; symptom reduction
   d. hospital use and costs; recidivism

29. The organization that functions both as a self-help group and political lobbying group for the mentally-ill is?
   a. National Organization for Mental Disease
 * b. The National Alliance for the Mentally Ill
   c. The American Psychological Association
   d. The American Psychological Society

30. To most Chinese, physical and psychological well being is dependent on the balance between _____ (female force) and _____ (male force).
 * a. Yin; Yan   c. gold; fire
   b. Yan; Yin   d. fire; gold

31. According to Hippocrates, the regulation of an individual's mental health was dependent upon the different _____.
   a. endorphins
   b. phlegm
 * c. humors
   d. meridians

32. Your friend appears quite depressed. According to Hippocrates this would be attributable to an excess of_____.
   a. phlegm
   b. humors
   c. blood
 * d. black bile

33. Hippocrates believed that great mood fluctuations were attributable to an excess of_____.
 * a. blood
   b. black bile
   c. yellow bile
   d. meridians

34. Following the collapse of the Roman Empire the primary explanations of mental illness were based upon _____.
   a. germ theory
   b. supernatural beliefs
   c. religious beliefs
   d. humanism
 * e. both b & c

35. During the _____, many mentally disordered individuals were subjected to "officially" sanctioned persecution.
   a. Renaissance
 * b. dark ages
   c. Ancient times
   d. none of the above

36. Please match the name with the appropriate term.......
   (b) Hippocrates   a. schizophrenia
   (e) Wah Torr   b. the Father of Western Medicine
   (c) Benjamin Rush   c. the Father of American Psychiatry
   (f) Phillipe Pinel   d. dementia praecox
   (a) Eugen Bleuler   e. the Father of Chinese Medicine
   (d) Emil Kraepelin   f. dementia

37. It was during the Renaissance that the idea of _____ was developed.
   a. disease
 * b. humanism
   c. community psychiatry
   d. community residences

38. Institutions developed during the 1600's to house the mentally disordered were known as _____.
   a. inpatient treatment centers
   b. community mental health centers
 * c. asylums
   d. jails

39. The United States established the first building to house the mentally disordered in the late _____.
   a. 1600s
   b. 1500s
   c. 1800s
 * d. 1700s

40. _____ was associated with the belief that people had certain inalienable rights and should be treated with dignity.
   * a. Humanism
   b. Community psychiatry
   c. Forensic psychology
   d. Social learning theory

41. The development of _____ or classifications of mental illness, led to the study of _____ or cause of mental illness.
   * a. nomenclatures; etiology
   b. etiology; nomenclatures
   c. diseases; nomenclatures
   d. zeitgeist; dementia

42. Nomenclature is to etiology as _____ is to _____.
   a. germ theory; schizophrenia
   * b. dementia; germ theory
   c. lobotomy; electric convulsive therapy
   d. disease; disorder

43. The impetus for a medical or biological explanation of mental illness can be traced to the recognition of_____ within the scientific community.
   a. humanism
   * b. germ theory
   c. psychotropic drugs
   d. genetics

44. The original mission of the American Psychological Association was specifically related to the issues of mental health and illness.
   a True   * b. False

45. During the late 1800s to mid 1900s, care of the mentally ill was the primary responsibility of _____.
   a. private hospitals
   b. religious organizations
   * c. the government
   d. the community

46. _____ argues that mental health patients should be treated using the least restrictive methods and in the least restrictive environment.
   * a. Community psychiatry
   b. Humanism
   c. The humanistic model
   d. The behavioral model

47. The mental health field devoted to the study of mental illness and crime is _____.
   a. community psychiatry
   b. social work
   c. clinical psychology
   * d. forensic psychology

48. Beginning in the 1960s, changes in the treatment of the mentally disordered included:
   a. the development of outpatient treatment centers
   b. the establishment of community residences
   c. the increased use of inpatient treatment centers
   d. all of the above
 * c. both a and b

49. It has been estimated that the largest proportion of mentally disordered individuals reside in _____.
   a. hospitals
   b. homeless shelters
 * c. nursing homes
   d. board-and-care-homes

50. _____ are community-based shelter-care facilities which include group homes and family care homes.
   a. Hospices
 * b. Board-and-care homes
   c. Community centers
   d. Recidivism

51. _____ is considered to be a typical measure of success for the evaluation of the effectiveness of deinstitutionalization.
   a. Social integration
   b. Recidivism
   c. Psychopathology
 * d. both a & b
   e. all of the above

52. Which of the following has been demonstrated to be an important environmental factor related to an individual's success following deinstitutionalization?
   a. population of city of residence
   b. depersonalization of services
   c. community attitudes
   d. both a & c
 * e. all of the above

53. _____ refer(s) to highly structured halfway houses for the mentally disordered stressing skill building and shared decision making.
   a. Residential treatment
   b. Empowerment communities
 * c. Lodge societies
   d. Assertive community treatment

54. Which of the following refers to case management models employing mobile treatment teams and assertive case management?
   a. Assertive community treatment
   b. Empowerment communities
   c. lodge societies
 * d. Assertive community treatment

55. Today many of the chronically mentally disordered reside in
    _____ as a primary means of care and shelter.
    a. nursing homes
    b. board-and-care homes
    c. mental hospitals
    d. family settings
  * e. all of the above

Identification of Terms

1. The broadening of responsibility for patient care from a single discrete service to multiple diverse services. [Answer=decentralization]

2. Legislation introduced to reduce the census of state hospitals and to provide treatment to maintain psychiatric patients in the community. [answer=Community Metal Health Act]

3. The longitudinal study investigating the prevalence of psychopathology from 1952 to 1960. [answer=Midtown Manhattan Study]

4. The philosophy associated with the field of community psychology is known as? [answer=empowerment]

5. Suggested to stand for a semantic mechanism to frame the complex, often conflicting, and sometimes unrelated sets of issues associated with mental health care reform. [answer=deinstitutionalization]

6. The focal points of acupuncture which facilitated the release of endorphins [answer=meridians]

7. The natural pain relievers located within the brian. [answer=endorphins]

8. The 1960's movement characterized by the sending of mentally disordered individuals back into the community. [answer=deinstitutionalization]

9. A subdiscipline of psychiatry advocating the least restrictive method of treatment in the least restrictive environment. [answer= community psychiatry]

10. A form of psychosis characterized by the deterioration of judgements, memory loss, and personality change. [answer=dementia]

Food For Thought

I. It has been suggested that the "deinstitutionalization" movement consists of several related perspectives. Discuss the three perspectives associated with mental health care reform. Discuss the two perspectives associated with the less than optimal effects of deinstitutionalization.

[Answer note= students should demonstrate knowledge of the philosophical, economical, and medical changes during this time. Furthermore psychological and sociological factors should be discussed in terms of their hindering effects to mental health treatment]

II. You have just been elected the president of the United States. The first priority is to reform the mental health care system of this country. What factors would want to consider when initiating the program's start? What factors would you want to consider in ensuring the plans success? [Answer notes= students should discuss issues relating to ethnic minority treatment, possible economic concerns, issues regarding after care treatment (outpatient) including case management]

III. "Deinstitutionalization" has had many meanings throughout its history. Discuss some of the ways in which others have described and perceived the reform of mental health care services. [Answer note= students should include in their discussion John Talbott's transinstitutionalization, popular literature reviews, and Bachrach's (1989) meaning and assumed processes]

IV. Different explanations and treatments of mental illness have been associated with different historical periods. Discuss some of the major historical perspectives of mental illness and how the mentally ill were treated during these times. [Answer notes: Discussion should include the dark ages, Renaissance, and delineation among the stages of the American mental health care reform. Students should demonstrate an understanding of the influences of the development of asylums, humanism, and germ theory (Psychotropic medication)].

V. Many of the programs developed by community psychologists have yielded variable results concerning their effectiveness in treating the chronically mentally ill. However, several model programs and "newer" approaches have demonstrated some success. Discuss the various model programs being implemented today in regards to their philosophies and methods of treatment. [Answer notes= students should include case management approaches including the Assertive community treatment]

<u>Key Terms</u>

Acupuncture
Assertive community treatment
Asylums
Board-and-care homes
Case management
Community Mental Health Act
Community psychiatry
Community residences
Deinstitutionlization
Dementia

Dementia praecox
Depersonalization of services
Electric convulsive therapy
Empowerment
Endorphin
Epidemiological Catchment Area Study
Etiology
Forensic psychology
Germ theory
Humanism
Humors
Inpatient treatment
Lobotomy
Lodge society
Meridians
Midtown Manhattan Study
Nomenclatures
Outpatient treatment
Psychotropic drugs
Recidivism
Residential treatment
Schizophrenia
Social integration
Transinstitutionalization
Yan
Yin
Zeitgeist

Recommended Films

<u>Schizophrenia: The Voices Within, the Community Without</u> (19 minutes). This program discusses the nature, symptoms, and medications used in the treatment of schizophrenia. Discussion concerning the deinstitutionlization of patients and difficulties encountered when releasing individuals with mental disorders back into the community is presented. Films for the Humanities & Sciences, P.O. Box 2053, Princeton, NJ 08543-2053.

<u>The Scandal of Psychiatric Hospitals: When the Goal Is Insurance Reimbursement</u> (52 minutes). This program shows how the mental health system has become a for profit industry catering to individuals with the best insurance plan. Specifically, this program shows how one group of hospitals herded up patients and held healthy Americans hostage. Program details efforts currently being made to return the fields of psychiatry and psychology to the roles of a healing profession. Films for the Humanities & Sciences, P.O. Box 2053, Princeton, NJ 08543-2053.

<u>Out of Sight</u> (60 minutes). This program outlines the history of the rise and fall of asylums and other institutions of the mentally ill beginning in the middle ages. Discuss the triumphs and brutalities of mental institutions and the current policies of deinsitutionalization. PBS Video Catalogue. 1320 Braddock Place, Alexandria, Virginia, 22314-1698.

<u>To Define True Madness</u> (60 minutes). This program examines the views of mental illness throughout the history of Western Society. Discussion

concerning issues of diagnoses and treatment is presented. PBS Video Catalogue. 1320 Braddock Place, Alexandria, Virginia, 22314-1698.

<u>Schizophrenics In The Streets</u> (28 minutes). A specially adapted Phil Donahue program which examines the results of emptying psychiatric facilities and putting patients back into society. Films for the Humanities & Sciences, P.O. Box 2053, Princeton, NJ 08543-2053.

CHAPTER 7

SOCIAL AND HUMAN SERVICES IN THE COMMUNITY

Introduction

The provision of assistance to those society has deemed as "less fortunate" has a varied history throughout civilization. Such variability has been demonstrated among the type of assistance provided, the benefactors of such assistance, and the philosophical underpinnings of assistance provision. The present chapter provides the student with an historical account of human service provision and a modern-day overview with particular emphasis placed on the issues of child-abuse, teenage pregnancy, the elderly, and the homeless.

Lectures and Notes

I. Historical Notes about Social Welfare in Western Society

Social welfare as conceptualized by Handel (1982), includes "a set of ideas and a set of activities and organizations for carrying out those ideas, all of which have taken shape over many centuries to provide people with income and other social benefits in ways that safeguard their dignity (p. 31)". Based on this conceptualization students are presented with an overview of both the ideological and practical aspects of social welfare programs.

Historically, there were three major forms of social welfare:
1. <u>Charity-philanthropy</u> - which refers to social welfare in which a donor or giver assists a recipient.
2. <u>public welfare</u> - which refers to social welfare in which the government assumes responsibility for individuals in need.
3. <u>mutual aid</u> - which refers to assistance provision with the goal of helping individuals to promote a level of self-sustenance.

However, criticisms concerning the use of public welfare and/or charity-philanthropy have included the variable definition of standard of living, the resulting social stigma for those who must demonstrate the need, and the differential status between donors and recipients. Thus, mutual aid type programs have received more attention and are believed to be the pre-cursors of modern day self-help groups.

Modern Forms of Social Welfare

Two modern forms of social assistance derived from the earlier models of social welfare and charity include **social insurance** and **social services**. Social insurance, developed during the time of the industrial revolution, is based on the premise of governmental responsibility for the poor. However, different from public welfare, social insurance involves the receipt of benefits that are earned by work. Examples include Social Security, Medicaid, and Food Stamps. Thus, individuals have either contributed to their benefits at one time or receive benefits contributed by those who are presently working.

Social services or public charity, is based upon the system of charity or philanthropy. Derived from the industrial revolution, social services include governmental assistance in a non-materialistic form maintained by the use of tax money. A major goal of social services is to ensure or maintain a productive work force by intervening or preventing social ills.

II. Social and Human Services in the 1990's

The breadth of human and social services provided both in the private and public sectors is vast. Given that, students are presented with an overview of one of the largest social welfare services provided by the government namely, **Medicaid**. However, prior to this overview students are presented with a discussion of what constitutes poverty. Poverty can be viewed as a multidimensional phenomena including financial constraints, feelings of hopelessness, and prejudice. Thus, one objective of medicaid is to assist individuals in moving from their present situation to a better life.

The overall evaluation of medicaid provision has resulted in the following findings:
* it is estimated that approximately 25% of all African- Americans are enrolled in medicaid
* the amount of money avaliable to the poor for spending has increased
* Whites have benefitted more than blacks in financial assistance

These findings suggest that although financial benefits have increased among those in need, the "differential effect" demonstrates other factors influencing the effectiveness of medicaid intervention. One possible explanation offered included the role of education. In other words, Medicaid assistance is useful only if people are educated enough to access it.

III. Specific Social Issues and Social Services

The student is presented with an overview of service provision for four specific populations. However, an equitable evaluation of the various services provided requires a consensus of standards. Students are presented with Price, Cowan, Lorion, and Ramos-McKay's (1988) five characteristics of model programs:
1. a specific target audience.
2. a goal of making a long-term and significant impact on the targeted groups, thus enhancing well-being.
3. the provision of necessary skills for the recipients to achieve their objectives.
4. the enhancement of natural support from family, community, and the school.
5. the inclusion of evaluative mechanisms to allow for the documentation of program outcomes.

Child Maltreatment

It is estimated that over 2.2 million children a year are subject to abuse. Abuse cases are often investigated by case workers from the Department of Social Services and may involve judicial intervention. Research has demonstrated several variables to be predictive of abuse including: prematurity of the infant, parental stress, low socioeconomic status, parent characteristics such as anxiety and defensiveness, and a lack of knowledge regarding child-rearing practices and skills. Furthermore, the effects of abuse on the recipient include an increased probability that he/she will become an abuser later in life, and an increased risk for emotional problems, and social, intellectual, and motoric delays.

Traditional intervention efforts have been attempted primarily at the individual clinical level. However, it has been argued that interventions at the national level, such as reducing unemployment and other stressors, may better assist <u>high-risk</u> groups before abuse occurs. Research assessing the efficacy of preventive programs for groups at risk for abuse have documented success. For example, the <u>Prenatal/Early Infancy Project</u> initiated by Olds et al., (1986) documented a 75% reduction in the incident of verified cases of child abuse and neglect over a comparison group. This program provided nurse home visitation to prevent a wide range of maternal and child health problems associated with poverty. Nurses carried out three major activities during the home visits: educating parents about fetal and infant development, promoting the involvement of family members and friends for social support and assistance in care of the infant, and developing a link between family members and other health and human services in the community. Thus, Old's work demonstrates that an expenditure of human and social service efforts can result in a productive, cost effective, and less destructive alternative than efforts initiated after the fact.

Another important finding which may enhance our understanding of the effects of abuse stems is that there are many children who are resistant to early trauma. Explication of the mechanisms involved in this resiliency and ability to cope may teach us important lessons regarding how to deal with abuse once it occurs.

Teenage Pregnancy

The United States has the highest teenage pregnancy rate relative to other Industrialized countries. More than one million teens become pregnant each year, and half of them give birth. It has been argued that one causal factor includes the social welfare system of this country. However, cross-national studies have demonstrated lower teenage pregnancy rates in industrialized countries with more comprehensive welfare programs than that of the United States. Thus, a direct causal link between pregnancy and welfare benefits has been not supported. Furthermore, Darity and Myers (1988) stated that a statistical inquiry does not indicate decisions about childbearing based upon monetary gains although, affectional reasons appear to be related. The absolute number of childbirths indicate a higher incidence among White adolescents. However, relative rates indicate a higher proportion of childbirths among Black adolescents. Criticism of the media has focused on the skewed attention paid to the latter statistic and the prevalent view of pregnancy as a female issue. Meyer, (1991) has pointed out the absence of White males in research and intervention strategies presented in the literature.

Preventive Programs

In contrast to the traditional individual level programs and the disappointing results of education-only preventive programs, wide range preventive efforts have demonstrated some success. An ecological approach which utilizes already existing environmental resources (i.e, teens' parents, schools) has been offered as a viable alternative to the individual therapy modality. However, complexities such as multiple perspectives of sexual behavior among family members, peers, and the community may diminish the overall effectiveness of such a preventive program.

Allen, Philliber, and Hoggson (1990), assessed under what conditions a school-based prevention program was most effective. The program, Teen Outreach Program of the Association of Junior Leagues, provided information on human development, life-option decision skills, and group support. Moreover the program emphasized volunteer community service. Results indicated that program participants had lower levels of suspension, school dropout, and pregnancy relative to similar others who did not participate. Older students appeared to benefit more when volunteer experience was emphasized, with younger students benefiting the most when the classroom component was intense. Thus, evidence supports a multifaceted approach to the prevention of school dropout, pregnancy, and other problems.

Secondary Prevention

When primary prevention programs fail, and teen pregnancy occurs, programs encouraging them to continue their educations and teaching parenting skills are needed. Such secondary prevention programs have included small academic classes augmented with counseling and prenatal health care services, and parenthood classes. Outcome research has demonstrated positive effects on academic achievement for teens who were poor students before becoming pregnant.

The Elderly

The elderly population has been consistently increasing in this country over time. It is estimated that by the year 2030, 20% of the population will be over the age of 65. However, the stereotype of the elderly as institutionalized feeble individuals is not supported by empirical investigations. Findings suggest only four to five percent of the elderly are institutionalized. Students are presented with the various issues confronting the elderly and attempts to ameliorate problems and enhance the quality of living during this portion of the life span.

Two frequent transitions often experienced by the elderly include the loss of health and the loss of a spouse. Research has shown such changes to be associated with;
* feelings of depression and increased stress
* perceived lack of control over health matters
* memory deficits and diminished mobility
* increased stress and demand on familial care providers.

Furthermore, ecological factors appear to play an important role in quality of life for the elderly. This includes whether such transitions involve relocation or major changes in living arrangements.

Of the many programatic efforts to assist the elderly, the student is presented with two major mechanisms postulated to facilitate a better quality of life and adjustment. The first social support, has been provided by means of informal networks, confidants, or other social support programs. However, studies assessing the efficacy of programs designed to offer social support indicate the perception of the individual providing the support is more important the support itself. In other words, factors such as reliability of sources, type of relationship, availability, and the "unnaturalness"of these relationships appear to be important factors in determining the effectiveness of the social support provided.

The second mechanism proposed includes the <u>sense of personal control</u>. Research has demonstrated positive effects for programs developed to enhance the sense of control in the elderly. An experiment conducted by Langer and Rodin (1976) demonstrated longer life spans, greater feelings of personal control, increased happiness, and activity levels, for nursing home residents who were given greater control over their daily living arrangements. Furthermore, these residents were given a plant to care for as a meanings of enhancing responsibility.

<u>Homelessness</u>

Many stereotypes concerning the homeless have been promulgated in the media and in political rhetoric. However, research demonstrates that many of today's homeless are victims of problems not created of their own accord. Thus, students are presented with some of the issues surrounding homelessness and community psychology's contribution to the amelioration of a very salient social condition.

Estimates for the number of homeless range from 200,000 to approximately three million. The wide range in estimates has been attributed to the heterogeneity within this group and the motivations of the particular agency supplying the estimate.

Research focusing on the "types" of homeless have yielded variable results. Morse, Calsyn, and Burger (1992) reported four types of homeless individuals: an economically disadvantaged, an alcoholic group, a mentally ill group, and an advantaged group. Rossi, proposes that the homeless can be divided into a <u>old</u> and <u>new</u> group. The "old" group refers to older, alcoholic men, residing in skid row hotels or houses. The "new" group refers to those who sleep on the streets or find public building to provide shelter from the weather. Statistics of today's homeless reveal the following:
* approximately 25% are women.
* there are approximately 750,000 homeless children.
* more are likely to be from minority groups.

Furthermore, studies have shown that homeless children have elevated levels of acute and chronic health problems and poorer nutrition. They are more likely to experience developmental delays such as short attention spans, speech delays, inappropriate social interactions, and psychological difficulties.

<u>Causes of Homelessness</u>

Research assessing the trajectory of the "path to homelessness" has demonstrated it to be quite heterogeneous. Thus, no particular cause or state has been consistently related to homelessness. Arguments concerning the varying causes have implicated mental illness, substance abuse, unemployment, lack of adequate housing, and poor housing opportunities. However, consistent differences among homeless and non-homeless groups have yet to be demonstrated.

A multidimensional perspective of homelessness has received some research support. For example, Weitzman et al., (1990) in a comparison between homeless and non-homeless families receiving public assistance, reported three distinct pathways that resulted in homelessness for particular families.

One pathway involved a stable housing situation which quickly deteriorated following a specific event (e.g. eviction). These families quickly descended into homelessness and may have benefitted from eviction-prevention programs. A second pathway involved a slow transition to homelessness. Characteristics of this path included frequent residency changes, landlord harassments, crowding, and concomitant substance abuse problems and domestic violence. Assistance recommendations included counseling programs concomitant to adequate housing supply. A third pathway described was associated with families who had never benefitted from a primary residence. This group included young mothers whose parents had themselves received public assistance. The authors suggest that ameliorative efforts should include job-skills and job relevant knowledge as well as possibilities for permanent housing.

Previous and current attempts for addressing homelessness have included increasing affordable housing, job training, and counseling. However, the overall efficacy of such programs has been questioned. Thus, presently new programs and approaches have been developed and are being implemented. Among those is the American Psychological Association's <u>pro bono</u> program. This program involves psychologist's providing services and training for the homeless and those volunteers assisting them.

A second approach to the solution of the homeless problem involves the use of federal legislation. For example, the passing of the McKinney Act established an Interagency Council on Homelessness. This is an effort to coordinate, monitor, and improve the federal response to the problems of homelessness. Furthermore, it is an attempt to reduce the duplication of services often demonstrated when independent charities or local governments are the primary coordinators of assistance. Overall, a coherent policy of federal legislation needs to pursue increased low-income housing, treatments for the mentally ill and substance abusing homeless, and education and job training for homeless individuals.

<u>Multiple Choice Questions</u>

1. _____ is a set of ideas, activities, and organizations for carrying out those ideas, to provide people with income and social benefits in ways that safeguard their dignity.
  a. Fund raising c. Social security
* b. Social welfare d. Welfare

2. Social welfare has been described as serving various concerns. Among those listed include:
  a. ideological c. social e. all of the above
  b. practical * d. both a & b

3. Ideological concerns related to the provision of social services (social welfare) include(s) perspectives from the _____ field(s).
  a. religious c. political e. all of the above
  b. economic * d. both a & c

4. The major form(s) of social welfare BEFORE modern times included
_____.
   a. charity   c. mutual aid   * e. all of the above
   b. public welfare   d. both a & c

5. A social welfare system in which a donor or giver assists a particular person is known as _____ .
   a. philanthropy   c. charity   e. all the above
   b. medicare   * d. both a & c

6. _____ refers to the situation in which the government assumes responsibility for the poor.
   a. Philanthropy   c. Social welfare
 * b. Public welfare   d. Social Security

7. Modern day "self help" groups are probably based on the early development of _____ as a form of social welfare.
 * a. mutual aid   c. charity
   b. communities   d. support groups

8. _____ is defined as the economic means of subsistence for an individual and sometimes is used as an indicator of need.
   a. Net income   * c. Standard of living
   b. Standard income   d. Income bracket

9. Critics of charity programs have argued that such programs
   a. are based on religious ideologue
   b. may result in creating social stigma
   c. have difficulty defining what constitutes "need"
 * d. all of the above

10. Contrary to previous beliefs, research has demonstrated that "helping" does Not result in differential status between the donor and receiver.
   a. True   * b. False

11. Related to mutual aid programs, _____ refers to the process by which individuals or groups are given the necessary skills to improve their own condition.
   a. welfare   c. charity
 * b. empowerment   d. social insurance

12. _____ is based on the premise of governmental responsibility for the poor using monies derived from taxes.
   a. Charity   * c. Social insurance
   b. Philanthropy   d. Social welfare

13. The difference between social insurance and other types of assistance programs is that social insurance is based on:
   a. charitable functions and organizations
 * b. benefit funds which have been previously earned by work
   c. community insurance groups operating independently of the government
   d. the provision of assistance to individuals who have not contributed to the overall process

14. Modern day social services are based upon the early philosophy of _____.
    * a. philanthropy   c. mutual aid
      b. public welfare   d. medicaid

15. Social services were developed with the goal(s) of;
    * a. maintaining a productive work force
      b. establishing a literate society
      c. stemming the spread of disease
      d. motivating the industrial revolution

16. _____ is considered to be today's most extensive public social welfare program.
      a. Social security   c. Welfare
    * b. Medicaid   d. Mutual aid

17. Poverty is best conceptualized as a phenomena consisting of_____.
      a. discrimination   c. hopelessness   * e. all of the above
      b. prejudice   d. a lack of money

18. Differences among racial groups regarding medicaid benefits have been attributed to _____.
      a. prejudice
      b. initial differences between groups
    * c. educational levels
      d. budget cuts

19. According to Price, Cowan, Lorion, and Ramos-McKay (1988), model programs are defined by possessing various characteristics including;
      a. targeting specific groups
      b. self-evaluative mechanisms
      c. grant support
      d. all of the above
    * e. both a & b

20. It is estimated that over _____ children a year are subject to abuse.
      a. 500,000   c. 10,000
      b. 1 million * d. 2 million

21. Factors associated with the occurrence of child abuse include:
      a. prematurity of the infant   c. parental stress
      b. low socioeconomic status   d. both a & c
                                    * e. all the above

22. Programs developed to prevent child abuse may benefit from including _____ as a part of a comprehensive program.
      a. medical care   * c. child-rearing practice
      b. psychotherapy   d. all of the above

23. Which of the following parental personality characteristics have been demonstrated to be associated with the tendency to abuse?
   * a. anxiety, defensiveness
   b. depression, anger
   c. anxiety, anger
   d. guilt, anxiety

24. Children who have been abused are at a higher risk for _____.
   a. becoming abusers later in life
   b. emotional problems
   c. motoric delays
   d. intellectual delays
   * e. all of the above

25. Traditional intervention efforts for child abuse cases usually involved the provision of _____ services at the individual level.
   a. medical   c. legal
   * b. psychotherapeutic   d. police

26. It has been argued that a more effective means of intervention for child abuse cases can be achieved through national policies directed towards:
   a. unemployment   c. income maintenance   * e. all the above
   b. child care   d. both a & c

27. One of the most successful child abuse prevention programs, the _____, documented a lower incidence of abuse and neglect.
   a. National Abuse Foundation
   * b. Prenatal/Early Infancy Project
   c. Save a Child
   d. Prenatal Recovery Program

28. The Prenatal/Early Infancy Project is an example of a successful _____ preventive program designed to address the problem of child abuse.
   a. secondary   c. tertiary
   b. remedial   * d. primary

29. Research has demonstrated that _____ can be an important factor in the prevention of abuse and assist those who are recipients once it has occurred.
   * a. social support   c. medicaid
   b. education   d. parental training

30. In a study conducted by Olds and his research team, _____ appeared to reduce the incidence of child abuse in those families participating in the study relative to non-participants.
   a. parental education
   b. increased child care involvement of family members
   c. providing a link between formal health and human services and family members
   d. both b & c
   * e. all of the above

31. Benefits of the child maltreatment interventions conducted by Olds and his research team included:
   a. the reduction in the number of verified cases of child abuse
   b. a decline in the number of emergency room visits for accidents and illnesses
   c. less punitive mother-child interactions
   d. both a & c
   * e. all of the above

32. Currently, _____ has the highest documented teenage pregnancy rate among Industrialized countries.
   * a. America   c. Japan
   b. France   d. Sweden

33. In the United States, the absolute number of teenage pregnancies is greatest among _____; however _____ demonstrate a relatively higher proportion.
   a. Blacks; Whites   c. Hispanics; Whites
   * b. Whites; Blacks   d. Blacks; Hispanics

34. The _____ approach to teen pregnancy prevention highlights the use of already existing environmental resources that may already be effective.
   a. secondary   c. sociological
   b. augmenting   * d. ecological

35. The ecological approach to teenage pregnancy prevention includes the utilizaton of the _____ surrounding the adolescent who may engage in sexual behavior.
   a. familial   c. environment   * e. all of the above
   b. social   d. both a & c

36. Which of the following represents a criticism of the research concerning teenage pregnancy?
   a. the exclusion of males
   b. the perception of teenage pregnancy being a minority issue
   c. the emphasis placed on the individual level of care or intervention
   d. both b & c
   * e. all of the above

37. According to research findings, teens' decisions about childbearing are primarily _____ in nature.
   a. monetary   * c. affectional
   b. impulsive   d. biological

38. Research has demonstrated a positive relationship between the comprehensiveness of a welfare program and the number of teenage pregnancies.
   a. True   * b. False

39. Which of the following is a popular reason given for teenage pregnancy?
   a. low self-esteem
   b. welfare programs
   c. low expectancies
   d. psychological problems
   * e. all of the above

40. Research findings have demonstrated sex education to be a strong factor in reducing teenage pregnancy and abortion rates.
   a. True   * b. False

41. Seitz, Apfel, and Rosebaum (1991) demonstrated a successful secondary prevention program for pregnant teenagers. The program provided _____ _____ services which increased overall academic performance for the participants.
   a. health care
   b. social
   c. educational
   d. both a & c
   * e. all of the above

42. It has been estimated that approximately _____ of the population will be over the age of 65 by the year 2030.
   * a. 20%
   b. 45%
   c. 10%
   d. 75%

43. Research has demonstrated that many of elderly in the United States:
   * a. reside in their own homes
   b. reside in the intensive care units of hospitals
   c. reside in nursing homes
   d. both a & b

44. It is estimated that approximately _____ of the elderly are institutionalized.
   a. 50%
   b. 10%
   c. 25%
   * d. 5%

45. _____ has/have been shown to be an important transition of aging for individuals which can have negative consequences such as depression and stress.
   a. Loss of health
   b. Loss of a spouse
   c. Loss of a job
   * d. both a & b
   e. all of the above

46. Research evidence suggests that environmental factors can influence the quality of life for the elderly. This has been demonstrated by:
   * a. married couples reporting wanting an energetic lifestyle
   b. greater quality of life ratings among the elderly in California
   c. a decrease in mortality rates among the elderly residing at home
   d. all of the above

47. In a study conducted by Heller et al., (1991), the _____ of social support appeared to be an important factor for explaining its possible effectiveness for the elderly.
   a. quantity
   b. frequency
   * c. quality
   d. all of the above

48. In a study conducted by Heller et al.(1991), the ineffectiveness of social support on fostering well-being among the elderly was attributed to _____.
    a. the perceived unreliability of the companions
    b. the novelty of the relationship
    c. the "artificial" nature of the relationship
* d. all of the above

49. Various programs designed to enhance _____ have been developed to assist and improve the quality of life for the elderly.
    a. social support   c. self-esteem
    b. personal control   * d. all of the above

50. According to Langer and Horn (1976), nursing home residents given a sense of _____ reported being happier and lived longer than residents in the non-intervention group.
    a. social support   c. self-esteem
* b. personal control   d. all of the above

51. Research has demonstrated that many of today's homeless are victims of _____ which can account for their current situation.
    a. drug abuse   * c. a lack of affordable housing
    b. mental illness   d. alcoholism

52. According to Rossi (1990), the _____ homeless are the type of homeless seen on the city streets after World War II and generally fit our stereotype of homelessness.
    a. "new"   c. "alpha"
* b. "old"   d. "beta"

53. Which of the following distinguished the two groups of homeless proposed by Rossi (1990).
    a. differing degrees of economic destitution
    b. differing ages
    c. different gender breakdowns
    d. different racial compositions
* e. all of the above

54. Research has demonstrated that homeless children are more likely to have _____ compared to children who are housed.
    a. acute and chronic health problems
    b. developmental delays
    c. psychological problems
    d. both a & c
* e. all of the above

55. Studies have demonstrated that homelessness is a(n) _____ condition for most individuals.
    a. chronic   * c. episodic
    b. involuntary   d. prolonged

56. Which of the following has been demonstrated to be an important factor in explaining the causes of homelessness for a majority of the homeless?
* a. structural variables   c. person-centered variables
    b. mental illness   d. unemployment

57. According to Weitzman et al. (1990), many families entering homelessness within a six month period demonstrated:
    a. relatively stable housing situations prior to becoming homeless
    b. multiple problems such as substance abuse and domestic violence
    c. a history of temporary housing and dependency on public assistance
    d. both b & c
* e. all of the above

58. Research has demonstrated that _____ alone provide(s) a strong intervention for homelessness.
    a. job training   b. employment
    c. both a & b   * d. Neither a nor b

59. Suggestions for addressing homelessness have included the increasing of _____.
    a. affordable housing   c. job training
    b. counseling   * d. all of the above

60. The _____ is a current piece of legislation which attempts to alleviate the homeless problem on the national level.
    a. APA *pro bono* program   c. Mutual Aid
* b. McKinney Act   d. Federal Assistance

Identification of Terms

1. A social welfare program in which a donor or giver assists a recipient or taker. [Answer= charity or philanthropy]

2. An indicator of need used by the government or agencies which characterizes the economic means of subsistence of an individual. [Answer= standard of living]

3. A public assistance program by which the government assumes responsibility for the poor based upon money earned by work. [Answer= social insurance]

4. One of the most extensive federal social welfare programs available to the poor. [Answer= Medicaid]

5. Ideas and activities that promote social good. [Answer= social welfare]

6. A nonmaterialistic human services program based on funds derived from taxes. [Answer= social services]

7. The type of homeless characterized by a younger age and larger proportion of woman and children. [Answer= new homeless]

8. Conceptualized as both a cause and effect of various problems which include hopelessness, prejudice, and discrimination. [Answer=poverty]

9. Based on the philosophy that individuals with similar problems can help each other. [Answer= self-help groups]

10. Established by the McKinney Act to coordinate, monitor, and improve the federal response to the problems of homelessness.
[Answer= Interagency Council on Homelessness]

Food for Thought

I. Social welfare programs have existed in some form throughout the history of western society. Until modern times there were three forms that differed in both their philosophies and methods of operation. Discuss the three major early forms of social welfare and give examples of current day programs based on their philosophies.

[Answer Notes= students should discuss the differences among charity/philanthropy, public welfare and mutual aid. Current day programs should include social services, medicaid, & self-help groups respectively]

II. Many arguments concerning the use of charity/philanthropy as a means to assist those "in need" have developed over the years. Discuss the issues surrounding the use of charity/philanthropy and the possible effects of such assistance.

[Answer Notes= students should discuss the difficulties of indicating need, differential status between the donor and recipient, and possible social stigma]

III. Evaluating the effectiveness of social service programs can pose a daunting task. However, having been appointed the chief community psychologist for your town you are now responsible for evaluating a particular community program. First listing, and then implementing the criteria proposed by Price, Cowan, Lorion, and Ramos-McKay (1988) describe how you would develop and evaluate a program designed to assist the abused children in your community.

[Answer Notes= students should demonstrate knowledge of the five model program criteria proposed by Price et al., (1990). These include a specific target audience, long-term significant impact, skill training, the strengthening of natural support, and the inclusion of evaluative mechanisms]

IV. Research has demonstrated that today's homeless are quite a heterogeneous group. Specifically, separate studies conducted by Morse, Calsyn, and Burger (1992) and Mowbray, Bybee, and Cohen (1993) identified four "types" of homeless. Discuss the four groups found for each study and outline how you would develop a program designed to address the needs of each group.

[Answer Notes= students should demonstrate knowledge of the economically disadvantaged group, alcoholic group, mentally ill group, and advantaged group outlined by Morse et al (1992). Furthermore, similar groups proposed Mowbray et al (1993) include a depressed group, hostile-psychotic group, substance abusers, and a "best functioning" group]

V. You have just received notification of your new job in a metropolitan nursing home. One of many of your responsibilities as a community psychologist is the development of a "quality of life" program for the residents in the nursing home. Describe some of transitional events the residents may have experienced and outline the specific variables which may enhance the effectiveness of your program.

[Answer Notes= students should include in their answer the possible loss of health and spouse as impactful transitions. Programs should include plans to foster sense of personal control, self-esteem, and social support]

Key Terms

Charity/philanthropy
Donor
Empowerment
Head Start
Job clubs
Medicaid
Mutual aid
New homeless
Old homeless
Poverty
Poverty line
Public welfare
Recipient
Self-efficacy
Self-help groups
Sense of (personal) control
Social insurance
Social security
Social service
Social welfare
Standard of living

Recommended Films

An Ounce Of Prevention (60 minutes). This program highlights several programs that are attempting to eliminate known risk factors (e.g., inadequate parenting skills, old age, and social isolation) that often lead to serious disorders. Corporation for Public Broadcasting, The Annenberg/CPB Project, 901 E Street, NW, Washington, DC, 20004-2037.

Addiction And The Family (19 minutes). This program examines the effects of a father's alcoholism on his family and the effectiveness of counseling in helping family members. Films for the Humanities & Sciences, P.O. Box 2053, Princeton, NJ 08543-2053.

Substance Abuse Among Latinos (28 minutes). This program looks at culturally specific approaches being generated within the Latino community to combat drug and alcohol use. Also, it examines the influence of familial, religious, and language factors on teaching within this community. Films for the Humanities & Sciences, P.O. Box 2053, Princeton, NJ 08543-2053.

The Culture Of Poverty (26 minutes). This program explores the emerging strategies for meeting the needs of children within the Latino culture. Films for the Humanities & Sciences, P.O. Box 2053, Princeton, NJ 08543-2053.

Homelessness Among Hispanics (28 minutes). This program looks at homelessness among Hispanics in San Francisco, San Antonino, and along the Texas-American border. Films for the Humanities & Sciences, P.O. Box 2053, Princeton, NJ 08543-2053.

Factors In Healthy Aging (28 minutes). This program reviews the impact of diet, smoking, family history, and personality on the aging process. Furthermore, programs developed to assess the predictors of healthy aging are highlighted. Films for the Humanities & Sciences, P.O. Box 2053, Princeton, NJ 08543-2053.

Nursing Home Care (19 minutes). This program highlights a well-run nursing home and describes its concerns. Films for the Humanities & Sciences, P.O. Box 2053, Princeton, NJ 08543-2053.

Caring For The Elderly (19 minutes). This program provides an overview of the various methods of care available for the aging, from day-care and group homes to respite and nursing homes. Films for the Humanities & Sciences, P.O. Box 2053, Princeton, NJ 08543-2053.

The Future of American Children: Policy Issues For The Year 2000 And Beyond (60 minutes). This program highlights the opinions' of experts regarding key issues facing policy makers and child advocates. Topics include child poverty, health policies, family preservation, and Headstart. PBS Adult Learning Satellite Service, 1320 Braddock Place, Alexandria, VA 22314-1698.

Child Abuse (19 minutes). This program deals with the delicate subject of sexuality and physically abused children. Discussion concerning the characteristics of offenders and the effects of abuse on the child is highlighted. Films for the Humanities & Sciences, P.O. Box 2053, Princeton, NJ 08543-2053.

Childhood Physical Abuse (26 minutes). This program covers the range of problems in the area of physical abuse of children including; the familial effects, criminal justice involvement, and various preventive efforts. Films for the Humanities & Sciences, P.O. Box 2053, Princeton, NJ 08543-2053.

CHAPTER 8

SCHOOLS, CHILDREN, AND COMMUNITY

Introduction

This chapter introduces to students the important interrelationships between home and school environments, as well as their joint impact on childhood development. The chapter begins by explicating Bronfenbrenner's ecological model. The nature of day care and its effects on child development are then discussed. The chapter then focuses on diversity and desegregation within schools. Head Start and other programs are discussed, as well as outcome data on their effectiveness. The distinction between short-term and follow-up research is emphasized. The authors discuss methods for enhancing acceptance within the classroom and community based programs for preventing school dropout. The authors conclude that community-oriented programs which incorporate parents, schools, and children will yield better results than traditional models which only focus on individual components.

Lecture and Notes

The Early Childhood Environment

The authors describe Bronfenbrenner's ecological perspective of childhood development, which emphasizes the interrelation between the home and school settings. In particular, the model describes a nested structure which has the home or school environment at the core. The next level consists of the ties between the core structures of school and home. The third level consists of environments in which children do not directly find themselves, but which still have an effect on children (e.g., parents' place of employment). An example of this last level is day care. This model emphasizes the impact of both the immediate and remote environments on human behavior. The remainder of the chapter uses practical examples to illustrate the utility of Brofenbrenner's model.

Day Care

Child day care can be defined as all the ways children are cared for when they are not being cared for by a nonemployed parent or during regular school classes. Day care services can come from licensed or unlicensed centers. Furthermore, service can come from family members, relatives, neighbors, or in-home sitters. In other words, there is no single, universal day care model.

With approximately 50% of all mothers working outside of the house, day care is a growing necessity in our society. Half of all preschoolers of employed mothers in the United States are in some form of nonfamilial care such as day care. Many other children care for themselves at home and are called "latchkey children."

Although many skeptics question the adjustment of children with working mothers, Gottfried and Gottfried's (1988) research indicates that the children of working mothers and fathers are not impaired. Furthermore, research by Scarr (1984) indicates that nonmaternal care has either no effect or slightly positive effects on cognitive development. Finally, one study conducted in Sweden found that family background and socioeconomic status were more important than type of child care in predicting social competency and ability to get along with peers. Taken together, these data suggest that being in day care does not have drastic effects on child development.

However, the quality of day care does have an important impact on child development and is the number one need of American families and children. High quality care is associated with enhanced language, cognitive, and social development, while poor quality care might be detrimental to development (Wasik et al., 1990). Unfortunately, research indicates that 60-90% of all family day care centers are unregulated, and thus quality of child care might be sacrificed. Regulations such as the "Federal Day Care Requirements" (FIDCR) were intended to prevent poor child care. However, these regulations are exempt from certain businesses, such as noncenter care facilities (e.g., private families) and organizations for children under 2-years old and handicapped children. Data indicate that businesses which follow FIDCR regulations have better staff-child ratios, more staff with child-related training, lower staff turnover rates, more age-appropriate classroom activities, and less harsh and more sensitive teachers. Also, nonprofit centers such as churches tend to have better quality care.

The authors review several possible remedies to the problems of quality care for children. First, greater federal regulation might ensure better care, although little progress is typically obtained this way. Second, parents could become more involved in school activities, although programs claiming parental involvement often get only minimal parent involvement. Third, high school students and senior citizens could participate in day care, as is typically done in Switzerland. Fourth, private businesses could offer on-site services to the children of employees either directly or through satellite learning centers. Thus, there are various options to improve the quality of care, although none is easy to implement.

Head Start and Related Programs

Many educators have argued that a rich childhood environment is essential for healthy childhood development. This model, sometimes called "naive environmentalism" was capsulized in the famous book by J. McVicker Hunt, <u>Intelligence and Experience</u>. This philosophy also guided the development of compensatory education programs, the most famous of which has been Head Start.

Head Start was initially established as part of the Economic Opportunity Act of 1964, targeting children between 3 and 5 years of age and from low income families. The program has a host of goals, including improving children's health and physical well-being, establishing expectations for success in the children, developing a responsible and constructive social attitude in children and their families, and increasing the self-worth of participants. These goals and others are reviewed in detail by the authors. The authors also distinguished Head Start from other programs. For example, Head Start was a broad, nationwide program. Second, it included a host of interventions, not just one. Third, the program was designed to ensure health screening and follow-up treatment. Most importantly, Head Start was not designed simply to enrich the children's environment. Rather, it was designed to enhance student motivation.

The authors then review the outcome and effectiveness of Head Start. First, the program was effective in getting medical services to needy children. However, the effects of the program on cognitive development were more complex. For example, children receiving services showed initial increases in "readiness to enter school" and I.Q. compared to control children not receiving services. However, the beneficial outcomes tended to be short lived and faded out within several years of schooling. Although some participants enrolled in Head Start received extended services (a programs called "Follow Through"), only a minority of schools across the country have adopted this program. On the other hand, compared to control groups, children receiving Follow Through services showed academic gains 4 to 5 years later. Also their family members were positively affected by the intervention. The authors also cite one longitudinal study (Jordon, Grallo, Deutsch, & Deustch, 1985) which followed the progress of Head Start and control children. Children receiving services had superior employment status, educational attainment, vocabulary skills, self-concept, and sense of self-control. The program also appears to be cost-effective. For every dollar spend on Head Start, society can save 4 to 7 dollars in remediation, welfare, and crime costs.

II. The Public Schools

Desegregation and Prejudice

The authors discuss the impact of psychologists on desegregation within the public schools, highlighting the 1954 Supreme Court case of Brown vs. The Board of Education. This famous case put an end to school segregation based on skin color, although the judges were concerned with neither the implementation nor the effects of their decision on children. As a result, some schools openly defied the court decision.

The authors then define and describe three related but distinct concepts: prejudice, discrimination, and stereotype:
(a) Prejudice is defined as an attitude (usually negative) toward the member of some group, based solely on their group membership.
(b) Discrimination involves prejudiced actions toward particular groups based almost solely on group membership.
(c) Stereotypes are beliefs that all members of certain groups share common traits or characteristics.

Unfortunately, even educated individuals can become prejudiced against others and subsequently discriminate in detrimental ways. As described by the authors, research by Rosenthal and Jacobson (1968) showed that teachers' beliefs about students, even if unfounded, can lead to self-fulfilling prophecies which influence student learning. In particular, the researchers found that students initially labeled as "bloomers" showed greater improvements in classroom learning and IQ than students initially labeled as "normal."

The authors point out that modern prejudice is covert and subtle, not easily detected by "direct" measurement. Researchers often need to look for respondents who "lean over backwards" in responses to detect modern racism.

Fostering Acceptance of Diversity in the Classroom

Given the diversity which exists within classrooms, how can teachers promote greater cohesion and acceptance among students? The authors discuss several techniques for accomplishing this:

(a) "Eye of the Storm" technique. Developed by teacher Jane Elliot, this method requires teachers to identify groups of children based on some physical attribute (e.g., eye color) and then take turns labeling each group as inferior to the other. Children then discuss their common feelings about being inferior.

(b) Increased intergroup contact. As argued by psychologist Stuart Cook, increased social contact reduces negative contact between groups only under five specific conditions, which are:
* equal status among groups/individuals
* attributes must become apparent so as to disconfirm prevailing stereotyped beliefs.
* contact situation must promote mutual independent relationship or cooperation to achieve a joint goal.
* details of group members must be revealed to encourage group members to be seen as individuals.
* social norms must favor group equality and egalitarian intergroup association.

(c) Jigsaw Classroom. Pioneered by Elliot Aronson and colleagues, students work on projects in mastery groups. At first, each group of students learn different skills. Eventually, new groups of students are formed with each group member bringing a new, valuable skill to his/her group. The jigsaw technique promotes cooperation rather than competition between students.

(d) Magnet schools. Magnet school bring together students from different schools who share common skills or talents (e.g., students speaking French). Research by Russell (1988) indicates that voluntary magnet schools promote greater long-term interracial exposure than mandatory school reassignment. This is because magnet schools discourage "White flight" from reassigned schools.

Effects of Desegregation on Academic Achievement

Early research conducted by Gerard and Miller (1975) conducted on the Riverside, California school district found detrimental effects of desegregation. Minority students were found to be less adjusted, selected less frequently as workmates, and demonstrated decreases in verbal achievement (especially in biased teachers' classrooms). However, these findings were not replicated in other studies. According to these authors, these discrepancies are due to:
a) lack of longitudinal studies.
b) too many correlational studies.
c) conditions necessary to facilitate intergroup contact are frequently not met.
d) studies are often reactive rather than proactive.

Long term follow-up research conducted by Braddock (1985) concludes that children attending desegregated schools attend desegregated colleges, have more White friends and work associates, earn higher incomes, and have higher job status. Thus, despite some initial reports, these data suggests beneficial effects of desegregation programs.

School Dropout

The authors report staggering dropout rates in American schools. The nationwide dropout rate is 20%. The rate is about 23% for Blacks, about 36% for Hispanics, and about 12% for Whites. However, others estimate dropout rates for Blacks ranging from 40-60%.

There are several factors that lead to dropout, including alienation from school, school failure, behavior problems in school, low socioeconomic status, English-as-second-language situations, insufficient learning materials at home, low self-esteem, and low feelings of personal control.

What can be done to reduce dropouts? Several things. Counseling to improve self-esteem or self-image is one option. Others have advocated an "ecological" approach to reduce the number of dropouts. The ecological approach considers the environmental factors such as the characteristics of the school as well as the individual who is about to drop out. For example, research stemming from an ecological orientation has demonstrated that middle-class students tend to drop out because of familial or behavioral problems, whereas lower class students drop out for academic and economic reasons. Along these lines, Fine (1986) identified poor school facilities and inadequate teaching staff as two school-related variables affecting student dropouts.

The authors describe in detail two intervention programs based on the ecological model: (a) the program by Felner and colleagues which trains homeroom teachers, and (b) HUGS, a comprehensive program including tutoring sessions and targeting students who are new parents. Data support the effectiveness of both programs.

School Climate

Feelings of alienation from school contribute to the dropout rate. Indeed, Sarason's book <u>Schooling in America: Scapegoat and Salvation</u> portrays American classrooms as unstimulating for children and teachers. Furthermore, one of this book's authors discusses her own research which indicates that the majority of students remembered negative, nonacademic school experiences (e.g., fights, fires, conflict) rather than positive school experiences. Some researchers argue that Americans schools need to follow the Japanese model of education, which gives more homework and has longer school days and school years. However, some research suggests that it is the Japanese home environment and not the school environment which is responsible for students' success (Stevenson & Lee, 1990).

Other researchers have proposed "alternative education" as a remedy to the dropout problem. Alternative education has students and their parents contribute to the school curriculum, smaller classes, and learning outside of the traditional classroom. Although the effectiveness of alternative education by higher student and teacher satisfaction and better school achievement, the mechanism of success is still unknown.

Finally, students should be familiar with other factors related to school (mal)adjustment. These factors include the following:

a) Students transferring from one school to another.
b) Poor cognitive problem-solving skills (in particular, poor skills for either interpersonal or school-related problems).
c) Readiness for school.
d) Divorce. Research by Sandler and colleagues (1988) indicates that divorce sometimes leads to decreased family income, decreased time with custodial and noncustodial parents, disruption in household routine, and less effective and positive parenting. However, other factors such as geographic distance and social support might moderate these effects.

Students should be familiar with the Children of Divorce Intervention Program, and the program designed by Stolberg and Garrison (1985), as examples of successful community type intervention programs for children at risk.

Multiple Choice Questions

1. Bronfenbrenner's ecological perspective of human development argued ...
   a. that the home and school settings are disconnected.
   b. that the "third layer" is the interrelationship between settings.
 * c. that structures (or settings) are nested.
   d. that the "inner most" layer is the environment that the child is not in.

2. Bronfenbrenner's model of human development is called the _____ perspective.
 * a. ecological
   b. nested
   c. interconnected
   d. developmental

3. According to Bronfenbrenner's model, advances in understanding development require investigation in ...
   a. actual environments.
   b. immediate environments.
   c. remote environments.
 * d. all of the above.

4. According to Zigler and Goodman (1982), day care is for ...
   a. children
   b. mothers
   c. fathers
 * d. all of the above

5. Child care providers...
   a. must be licensed.
 * b. can be licensed or unlicensed.
   c. cannot be relatives or family members of children receiving day care services.
   d. none of the above is true.

6. According to the book, approximately _____ of all preschoolers of employed mothers in the United States receive some form of nonfamilial care.
   a. 25%
* b. 50%
   c. 75%
   d. 85%

7. According to the book, approximately _____ of all mothers work outside of the home, and this estimate is expected to _____.
* a. 50% ; increase
   b. 50% ; decrease
   c. 30% ; increase
   d. 30% ; decrease

8. Which of the following statements is true?
   a. Gottfried and Gottfried's (1988) review concluded that children's adjustment suffered when both parents were employed.
   b. latchkey children usually receive day care services.
* c. when conducting research on child development, it is important to control for family and socioeconomic backgrounds of the children.
   d. child care services include "for-profit" centers, but do not include "not-for-profit" centers.

9. Which of the following is typically a "not-for-profit" child care center?
   a. church-sponsored centers
   b. family-based care
* c. both a and b
   d. neither a nor b

10. A study conducted in Sweden examined the social skills of children receiving various types of child day care. The authors of this study concluded that...
* a. family background and socioeconomic status were better predictors of social competency than type of child care.
   b. type of child care was a better predictor of social competency than family background or socioeconomic status.
   c. neither the type of child care nor the family background/socioeconomic status predicted social competency.
   d. social competency could not be measured.

11. According to Gamble and Zigler (1986)...
   a. poor day care quality has equally bad effects on wealthy and poor children.
* b. poor day care quality has worse effects on poor children than wealthy children.
   c. poor day care quality has worse effects on wealthy than poor children.
   d. the number of negative stressors in a child's environment is unrelated to the quality of his/her day care services.

12. Kamerman and Kahn (1987) found that _____ of all family day-care homes are unregulated.
    a. 10%-25%
    b. 25%-50%
    c. 50%-75%
    * d. 60%-90%

13. What organization was formed in 1968 to prevent poor child care?
    * a. Federal Interagency Day Care Requirements
    b. Day Care Federal Regulatory Board
    c. Federal Guidelines for Child Care Regulations
    d. none of the above

14. Which of the following statements about the FIDCR is true?
    * a. its regulations do not include provisions for noncenter care.
    b. its regulations include provisions for children under 2 years old.
    c. its regulations include provisions for handicapped children.
    d. its regulations for child care centers are clearly delineated.

15. Phillips, Howe, and Whitebook (1982) examined the effects of regulation on quality of care. They found that more stringent regulations had positive effects on which of the following?
    a. staff-child ratios
    b. child-related training of staff
    c. staff turnover rate
    * d. all of the above

16. Research by Phillips and colleagues (1982) found that ...
    a. "for-profit" centers offered better quality care than "nonprofit" centers.
    * b. "nonprofit" centers offered better quality care than "for-profit" centers.
    c. "nonprofit" and "for-profit" centers offered comparable quality care to their children.
    d. churches offer too little space and are too inconveniently located to function as centers.

17. Zigler and Turner (1982) conclude that day care centers which promote "parental involvement" at their centers...
    a. have parents who actually spend a good amount of time at the centers.
    b. have parents who work fewer hours per week in order to be involved with the child care center.
    * c. have parents who are, in actuality, only minimally involved in the center.
    d. both a and b are true.

18. Which country has a law indicating that facilities for the elderly must be built adjacent to or share facilities with a day-care center, school, or other institution serving children.
    a. France
    * b. Switzerland
    c. Spain
    d. Canada

19. John is an employee for a large corporation. This corporation has a special facility for John's daughter who is in kindergarten. This facility is only for small children whose parents work for the corporation. We would call this facility which of the following?
   a. compensatory education
   b. a jigsaw classroom
 * c. a satellite learning center
   d. Head Start

20. _____ are designed to assist disadvantaged children.
 * a. Compensatory education
   b. Jigsaw classrooms
   c. Ecological perspectives
   d. none of the above

21. Approximately what percentage of the children placed in classes for the educable mentally retarded are African-American?
   a. 20%
 * b. 40%
   c. 60%
   d. 80%

22. According to Starfield (1982) family income is more strongly related to _____ than any other sociodemographic characteristic.
   a. type of child care services
   b. years of education
 * c. health status
   d. none of the above

23. Poor children are ____ more likely to miss school because of illness and to have these problems interfere with their school work than children from affluent families.
   a. 10 times
   b. 20 times
   c. 30 times
 * d. 40 times

24. Head Start attempts to meet children's _____ needs.
   a. emotional
   b. health
   c. educational
 * d. all of the above

25. According to research by Kozol (1990), Head Start reaches _____ eligible children.
 * a. 1 out of 5
   b. 2 out of 5
   c. 3 out of 5
   d. 4 out of 5

26. Head Start ...
    a. attempts to use one single intervention program to help all eligible children.
  * b. is a nationwide program.
    c. discourages parental involvement in programs.
    d. was designed to change children's environments but not their motivation levels.

27. Which of the following statements about the High/Scope Perry Preschool program is true?
    a. The program views children as active, self-initiating learners.
    b. Children in the program select their own activities from a variety of learning areas prepared by the teacher.
    c. The program includes staff trained in early childhood development and parental involvement.
  * d. all of the above are included in the program.

28. Based on research, which of the following statements about the outcome of Head Start is true?
    a. The program was not effective in getting medical services to needy children.
    b. Children enrolled in Head Start and those not enrolled in Head Start showed no differences in "readiness to enter school."
  * c. The positive effects of Head Start on I.Q. were short-lived.
    d. Children enrolled in Head Start showed increases in both I.Q. and behavior problems. Neither of these increments went away over time.

29. According to research by Seitz and colleagues (1977), children enrolled in Head Start/Follow Through...
    a. had parents positively effected by the program.
    b. had siblings positively effected by the program.
    c. showed academic gains which lasted for four to five years.
  * d. all of the above are true.

30. Jordon and colleagues (1985) conducted longitudinal research by finding 70 adults who had previously participated in early education programs, as well as 70 control subjects who had not participated in such programs. The authors found that participation in early education programs...
    a. led to greater educational attainment and job status, but only among women.
  * b. led to greater educational attainment and job status, but only among men.
    c. had no impact on educational attainment or job status.
    d. led to greater vocabulary skills and self-concept, but only among women.

31. Individuals who had participated in the Perry Preschool Program ultimately...
    a. had worse grades in secondary school than nonparticipants.
    b. had less job satisfaction than nonparticipants.
  * c. had fewer arrests than nonparticipants.
    d. all of the above are true.

32. For every dollar spent on early intervention, society can save _____ dollars in costs for remediation, welfare, and crime.
   a. 1-2
   b. 3-5
 * c. 4-7
   d. 8-11

33. Which of the following was no longer tolerated in American schools as a result of Brown vs. Board of Education of Topeka, Kansas.
   a. fully segregated classrooms
   b. separate but equal educational facilities
   c. separate classrooms for Black and White students
 * d. all of the above were no longer tolerated

34. Judges in the case of Brown vs. the Board of Education...
   a. were initially concerned with the precise effects of their decision on children.
 * b. were not initially concerned with how their decision would be implemented.
   c. allowed for separate but equal educational facilities.
   d. all of the above are correct.

35. _____ is an attitude toward the members of some group, based solely on their group membership.
   a. Racism
   b. Discrimination
 * c. Prejudice
   d. Stereotype

36. Your classmates decide not to let you join their soccer club because you are Jewish. This is an example of ...
   a. Stereotype
 * b. Discrimination
   c. the contact hypothesis
   d. Modern Prejudice

37. Paul believes that all Native Americans are alcoholics and smoke pipes. This is an example of ...
 * a. a stereotype
   b. prejudice
   c. discrimination
   d. self-fulfilling prophecy

38. Rosenthal and Jacobson (1968) conducted research on "bloomers" and "normal" children. Their data indicated ...
   a. that a self-fulfilling prophecy had occurred.
   b. Teachers' expectations influenced student performance.
   c. "bloomers" showed dramatic improvements in classroom performance and I.Q. scores.
 * d. all of the above are true.

39. Modern prejudice involves attitudes that are...
   a. overt
 * b. covert
   c. derived from the media
   d. formed only in industrialized cultures

40. Your teacher tells you that children with red hair are inferior and should be ignored. One week later, she indicates that children with brown hair are inferior and should be ignored. This technique is called...
   a. a jigsaw classroom
   b. intergroup contact
 * c. The Eye of the Storm
   d. modern prejudice

41. The contact hypothesis states that ...
   a. intergroup conflict can be resolved merely by bringing "enemy" groups together.
   b. in order for intergroup contact to reduce conflict, the two groups must not have equal status.
 * c. in order for intergroups contact to reduce conflict, the group members must be seen as individuals.
   d. joint goals and cooperation between groups can make conflict even worse between "enemy" groups.

42. Elliot Aronson pioneered a technique to help students get along in the classroom. His technique involves the use of "mastery groups" and is known as...
 * a. the jigsaw classroom
   b. the Eye of the Storm
   c. the contact hypothesis
   d. magnet schools

43. You are an excellent guitar player. Therefore, your parents send you to a special school with students from other districts who also love music. This type of school (classroom) is know as ...
   a. a jigsaw classroom
 * b. a magnet school
   c. Help Us Guarantee Success (HUGS)
   d. compensatory education

44. Initial studies on the effects of desegregation by Gerard and Miller (1975) concluded that...
   a. minority students were better adjusted than White students.
   b. minority students were frequently selected as workmates.
 * c. students in the classrooms of biased teachers showed the greatest drops in verbal achievement scores.
   d. all of the above are true.

45. Studies examining the effects of desegregation often yielded inconsistent findings. According to the text, this is due to which of the following factors?
 * a. Few studies were longitudinal
   b. Few studies were correlational
   c. Most studies were proactive and not reactive
   d. Conditions necessary for intergroup contact were usually met in previous studies.

46. Braddock (1985) studied the long-term effects of desegregation. He found that African-Americans attending desegregated schools...
    a. were more likely to attend desegregated colleges
    b. had more White friends and work associates
    c. earned higher incomes
  * d. all of the above

47. By the year 2000, _____ of all school children will be minority.
    a. one quarter
  * b. one third
    c. one half
    d. three quarters

48. The nationwide dropout rate is _____ for Hispanic students and _____ for White students.
  * a. 36% ; 12%
    b. 23% ; 12%
    c. 12% ; 36%
    d. 40% ; 5%

49. Which of the following factors lead to drop out?
    a. alienation from school
    b. low socioeconomic status
    c. English as a second language
  * d. all of the above

50. Middle class students drop out of school because of _____ problems, whereas poor students drop out of school because of _____ problems.
    a. economic ; behavior
  * b. family ; economic
    c. behavior ; family
    d. academic ; economic

51. Felner and colleagues (1991) have developed a prevention program for students at risk for dropping out of school. Their program redefines the role of the _____ to provide counseling and guidance to students.
  * a. homeroom teachers
    b. principals
    c. parents
    d. school nurses

52. HUGS was developed to assist students who...
    a. were new parents
    b. felt that they were being ignored in school
    c. were having academic difficulties in school
  * d. all of the above

53. Seymour Sarason's book <u>Schooling in America: Scapegoat and Salvation</u> argues that...
    a. American education is interesting to teachers but not students.
    b. Children learn faster inside than outside of the school.
  * c. Schools are uninteresting for both students and teachers.
    d. American education is interesting to students but not teachers.

54. Research by one of the book authors (KD) found that most of her students recalled _____ events when asked to recall their most memorable school experience.
* a. negative nonacademic
  b. positive nonacademic
  c. negative academic
  d. positive academic

55. Research by Stevenson and Lee (1990) indicates that the success of Asian school students is due to ...
  a. their longer school days.
  b. the larger amount of homework assignments they receive.
  c. their longer school year.
* d. their home environments.

56. Which of the following factors explains the reported success of "alternative education?"
  a. student empowerment
  b. empathic teachers
  c. student participation
* d. all of the above

57. Which of the following is not an example of "interpersonal cognitive problem-solving?"
  a. Paul has to learn how not to get into fights with other classmates.
* b. Mary has to learn how to walk home after school without getting lost.
  c. Joe has to learn to assert himself to his classmates so that he is not ignored.
  d. Carla has to learn how to generate and evaluate a variety of possible solutions for dealing with her parents.

58. The effects of divorce on children may be moderated by which of the following factors?
  a. geographic distance from the home
  b. family support
  c. chum support
* d. all of the above

59. Which of the following statements is true?
  a. Under high levels of stress, children receiving support from nonfamily adults were less well adjusted than children receiving no support.
  b. Under low levels of stress, children receiving support from nonfamily and family adults were better adjusted than children receiving no support.
* c. Under low levels of stress, children receiving support from nonfamily adults were less well adjusted than children receiving no support.
  d. No matter what type of stress, children benefit from any type of social support from adults that they can receive.

60. Braver (1990) studied the number of divorced families taking advantage of available program interventions. Braver concluded that...
   a. when programs are available, most people will take advantage of them.
 * b. even when programs are available, not everyone can or will participate in them.
   c. most families never become fully eligible for program interventions.
   d. most families which start intervention programs also finish them in their entirety.

Identification of Terms

1. Compensatory education program established under the Economic Opportunity Act of 1964. (Answer=Head Start).

2. Children who go home by themselves after school. (Answer=Latchkey children).

3. Beliefs that all members of certain groups share common traits or characteristics. (Answer=Stereotype).

4. Negative attitudes toward the members of some group, based solely on their group membership. (Answer= Prejudice).

5. Phenomenon whereby one's beliefs and expectations about others ultimately leads others to behave in accordance with these expectations. (Answer= Self-fulfilling prophecy).

6. Prejudices which are covert and subtle. (Answer= Modern prejudice).

7. Classroom technique in which students from various "mastery groups" are ultimately brought together to share information. (Answer= Jigsaw classrooms).

8. Generation and evaluation of alternative strategies for reaching personal goals. (Answer= Cognitive problem-solving).

9. A lasting change in the way in which the individual perceives and deals with the environment. (Answer= Development).

10. A set of nested structures, one inside of another, depicting the relationship between the student, the classroom, and the home environment. (Answer= Ecological setting).

Food For Thought

I. Imagine that you are a famous community psychologist trying to convince administrators of a day care center to do longitudinal research with follow-up data. Define the difference between short-term and longitudinal research. Using examples from the desegregation and Head Start literature, explain how short-term and longitudinal research can yield different results. Why do many people prefer short-term research?

II. What are the remedies to the day-care dilemma in the United States. Which one's do you favor and which ones do you reject? Which ones seem most and least feasible to implement in contemporary society?

[Answer notes: Discuss issues such as federal interventions, parental involvement, companies, senior citizens, etc.]

III. Give an example of "traditional prejudice" and "modern prejudice" as related to (a) racism and (b) sexism.

IV. According to Cook (1985), what are the five conditions necessary for intergroup contact to reduce prejudice. List the conditions and give concrete examples for each one.

V. Imagine that you are requested to help a nine year old girl who is afraid of approaching other children in school to talk. How would you help her using (interpersonal) cognitive problem-solving skills? Be specific! That is, list at least five specific alternative responses she could make to help her interact better. Based on research by Elias and colleagues (1986), what might be the long-term effects of your intervention if it is successful?

[Answer notes: Sample alternative responses include thinking about how fearless children would act, watching talkative children speak out in class, placing the child in a group which encourages talking out load, teaching the child to take slow deep breaths before talking, teaching the child to remain focused on what she is saying, etc.]

Key Terms

Alienation from school
Alternative education
Child day care
Cognitive problem-solving
Compensatory education
Contact hypothesis
Development
Discrimination
Ecological environment
Head Start
Intergroup contact
Interpersonal cognitive problem solving
Jigsaw technique
Latchkey children
Longitudinal research
Modern prejudice
Prejudice
Readiness
Satellite learning centers
Self-fulfilling prophecies
Stereotypes

Recommended Films

America's Schools: Who Gives A Damn? (Part II) (60 minutes). Panel discussion on a number of social problems which work their ways into the public school, including poverty, drugs, crumbling families, and racial tensions. PBS Video, 1320 Braddock Place, Alexandria, VA 22314-1698. Fax: 703-739-5269.

Are Our Public Schools Beyond Repair? (60 minutes). Consumers and critics square off against education professionals to determine how schools should be restructured and by whom. PBS Video, 1320 Braddock Place, Alexandria, VA 22314-1698. Fax: 703-739-5269.

Beyond Hate (88 minutes). Psychologists explore the economic basis of hate and its psychological mechanisms. The program also illustrates a high school conflict-resolution class and a discussion between a Holocaust survivior and young children about the dangers of stereotyping. PBS Video, 1320 Braddock Place, Alexandria, VA 22314-1698. Fax: 703-739-5269.

Ethnic Notions (56 minutes). Voyages through American social history to document the evolution of deeply rooted stereotypes about African Americans. Presents caricatures that permeated popular culture from the 1820's through the civil right's era. Insight Media Inc., 2162 Broadway, New York, New York, 10024. Fax: 212-799-5309.

Family In Crisis (28 minutes). Special episode of Phil Donahue show focusing on the plight of poor children growing up in single-parent households. Films For The Humanities, Inc. P.O. Box 2053, Princeton, N.J. 08543-2053. Fax: 609-275-3767.

The Future of American Children: Policy Issues For The Year 2000 and Beyond (60 minutes). This program addresses the vast problems facing underprivileged children, including health care issues and day care. A panel of experts looks at possible solutions to these issues for the next century, including Head Start, foster grandparents, and elder mentor programs. PBS--Adult Learning Satellite Service, 1320 Braddock Place, Alexandria, VA 22314-1698. Fax: 708-739-8495.

Latchkey Families (23 minutes). This program offers specific guidance to working parents with children who are on their own after school. Interviews conducted with educational and law enforcement specialists. Films For The Humanities, Inc. P.O. Box 2053, Princeton, N.J. 08543-2053. Fax: 609-275-3767.

Paid To Care (30 minutes). This program highlights three family day care providers and emphasizes the need for day care to be viewed as a three-way partnership between providers, parents, and the government. PBS Video, 1320 Braddock Place, Alexandria, VA 22314-1698. Fax: 703-739-5269.

On Hate Street (48 minutes). This 48-Hours episode examines the growth of hate groups and hate crimes in the United States. Includes segments on the Ku Klux Klan, a riot on Martin Luther King's birthday, the Holocaust, and hate crimes against homosexuals. Insight Media Inc., 2162 Broadway, New York, New York, 10024. Fax: 212-799-5309.

Prejudice (30 minutes). Showing scenarios of prejudiced behavior that involve racial, gender, and social class bias, this program explores stereotypes and emotions underlying prejudice and discrimination. Insight Media Inc., 2162 Broadway, New York, New York, 10024. Fax: 212-799-5309.

Prejudice: The Eye Of The Storm (25 minutes). Documentary about a third-grade teacher's classroom experiment which resulted in broken friendships, feelings of frustration and anger, and discriminatory behavior. Insight Media Inc., 2162 Broadway, New York, sNew York, 10024. Fax: 212-799-5309.

Understanding Prejudice (90 minutes). Psychiatrist Price M. Cobb explains how prejudice and stereotyping are natural functions developed for coping with a threatening environment. Illustrates ethnotherapy, a technique for examining the way people think about other ethnic groups. Insight Media Inc., 2162 Broadway, New York, New York, 10024. Fax: 212-799-5309.

CHAPTER 9

LAW, CRIME, AND THE COMMUNITY

Introduction

The increasing prevalence of criminal activities reported both in the community and media has been associated with a concomitant call for more political involvement. Given both the political and social complexities surrounding such an issue, community psychology may offer important insights facilitating better prevention services. The present chapter provides an overview of the criminal justice system and discusses the various programs designed by community psychologists addressing the myriad of needs of those involved with the criminal justice system.

Lectures and Notes

I. <u>The Traditional Justice System Criminal Justice Processes</u>

The traditional criminal justice system is multilayered consisting of law enforcement agencies (police), various courts (eg., municipal, state, federal, civil), prisons, and departments such as probation and parole. Discussion regarding the manner in which such organizations interact will provide the student with a basis with which to compare the reforms discussed in the latter half of the chapter. Such reforms may be discussed within the context of the calls for increased involvement by community psychologists to examine the situational and environmental factors contributing to criminal behavior.

An individual's initial introduction to the criminal justice system may involve an arrest, an indictment (officially charged with the crime), and an arraignment (addressing the charge). Students should be introduced to the arguments surrounding plea bargaining.

<u>Crime and Criminals</u>

Although frequently discussed, what actually constitutes a crime is inextricably related to the laws of a particular society. As such, societal and historical differences hinder a consensual and concrete definition of crime. However, a rudimentary definition of crime has been presented as <u>an intentional act that violates the prescriptions or proscriptions of the criminal law under conditions in which no legal excuse applies and where there is a state with power to codify such laws and to enforce penalties in response to their breach.</u>

This definition holds:
- that there is no crime without laws and without a state to punish a breach of such laws
- there is no crime without intention
- there is no crime where the offender is deemed incompetent
- there is no crime where an act that would otherwise be offensive is justified by law

Defining what constitutes a crime has been a challenge both from a political and philosophical perspective. However, further complexities are

introduced when hypothesizing about the incidence rate and possible causes of criminal behavior. Students should be introduced to the various methods of measuring or recording crime and the variables associated with population based assessments of crime. Discussion topics may center on the following research findings:
* research demonstrating violent crimes are twice as likely to be reported than nonviolent.
* men in the United States are more likely to die in a homicide than the men of many other countries
* a greater homicide rate among African-American males.

Theories of why homicides are greater in number in this country have focused on among others the availability of guns. Cross-national surveys find associations between number of handguns and homicide rates. However, cross-national surveys and comparisons must also consider other variables such as ethnic homogeneity, history of racial conflict, and the obedience to authority, before concluding gun control within a particular nation causes fewer handgun deaths.

Statistics show that young African-American males have the highest death rates from homicides particularly when committed by other African-American males. Postulated reasons for Black-on-Black violence have included poverty, frustration and blocked opportunities, and prejudice. Students should be aware of the current evidence for these proposed causes.

The Prisons

Based on the philosophy of retribution rather than rehabilitation, the criminal justice system is responsible for the supervision of approximately one of every 46 adults (or 4.1 million). This includes incarceration, probation, and parole.

Recidivism rates are approximately 43% within the first three years of release and it has been argued that prisons are total institutions, that is, the handling of an individual's diverse needs through bureaucracy. Students should be informed of the conditions surrounding imprisonment including overcrowding, the economic effects, psychological effects, and the imaginative methods for addressing such difficulties.

Victims and Fear of Being Victimized

Community psychologists are interested both in the fear of crime and the actual victimization. Some studies have found that those most fearful of crime are sometimes the least likely to be victimized. Examples include;
* Young men are the least afraid of violent crime although are the most likely to be victimized
* Young women fear crime more than young men but are less likely to be victimized
* Elderly women are most fearful yet the least likely to be victimized

Several theories have been proposed to explain this phenomenon or fear-victimization paradox. They include;
* The perception of urban environments as dangerous and their deterioration signalling the erosion of social

controls
* Taylor and Shumaker's (1990) proposal that individuals in
  high crime areas become desensitized to the probability of
  crime

Furthermore, Taylor and Shumaker propose that crime can be conceptualized as a natural disaster. This has led to the recommendation of a <u>social problems orientation</u> to crime prevention. Such an orientation supported by other community psychologists stresses the need for a "fit" between the particular neighborhood, the residents, and the specific preventive program.

Community psychologists are also interested in the treatment of actual victims. Topics for class discussion can include
* the frequent exclusion of victims from the legal
  process.
* findings suggesting that sexual assault victims are subjected
  to more negative questioning and are required to give
  more personal revealing testimony.
* the difficulty for victims collecting their awards from
  civil cases.

The difficulty encountered by many victims may be associated with the more than 4,000 victim assistance programs in the United States.

<u>Enforcement Agencies</u>

The primary means of law enforcement within this country involves the police department. However, increasing evidence indicates numerous difficulties associated with the policing of communities. Furthermore, there has been increased interest in police burnout and the frequency of murdered police. Discussion of the issues surrounding the policing of a community should include;
* the differing views of what should constitute the need for
  police intervention.
* the police involvement in domestic disputes and the
  handling of the mentally ill despite limited training
  for such situations.
* differing views of the "type" of policing style which
  may be most effective.

An associated question concerning policing matters involves the efficacy of enforcement and police presence within the community. Research results appear to support the use of police enforcement agencies for the reduction in the incidence of crime.

II. <u>Addressing Diverse Justice System Needs with Community Psychology</u>

Increasingly, professionals and lay persons are asked to make decisions based, either explicitly or implicitly, on the ability to predict the occurrence of criminal behavior. However, research findings suggest that laypersons are often wrong and tend to err in the direction of false positives (Marquart, Ekland-Olson, & Sorensen, 1989). Class discussion should focus on the implications of these findings concerning the assigning of sentences by jurors.

A further and maybe more important question concerns the ability of psychologists and other professionals to predict individuals "at risk" for engaging in criminal behavior. In general, research evidence suggests that professionals can with some accuracy forecast those who may be at-risk for breaking the law. Class discussions can focus on such findings as:

* Crimes were more likely to be committed by youths with prior convictions and who were unemployed (Roesch, 1988)
* Familial characteristics such as low-conflict, high-religiousness, and strong-cohesiveness were related to lower delinquency rates (Tolan & Lorion, 1988).
* Crime-prone peer affiliation is related to an increased probability of delinquency or repeat offenses upon release from youth detention centers (Coates, 1981).
* The high prevalence rate of childhood trauma (i.e sexual abuse) among female delinquents (Bowers, 1990).

Prevention Focused Programs

Given a broad research base, community psychologists have set forth to develop innovative crime prevention programs. Students should be made aware of the various individual, environmental, and social variables targeted by preventive programs. Research evidence suggests the following variables are important for preventive efforts targeting:

At-Risk Individuals

* Interventions should be focused at the youth's social network, including peers, parents, and role models (Coates, 1981).
* Individuals should be included and participate in the decision-making process (Martin & Osgood, 1987)
* The use of after-school activities and classroom sessions to prevent gang membership (Thompson & Jason, 1987)

The Environment

Increasing evidence suggests that environmental characteristics are associated with the incidence of criminal activities. Students can discuss the various environmental changes which may help reduce the probability of criminal activities. Discussions may focus on the implications of documented research findings such as:

* a relation between ambient temperature increases and aggression (Anderson & Anderson, 1984)
* the relationship between crowding and both negative affect and various behaviors (Baron & Byrne, 1993).
* the influences of location in neighborhood, parking lot size, and number of hours open, on store robberies (Stolzenberg, 1990).
* the decreased vulnerability of easily surveyable houses to robbery (MacDonald & Gifford, 1989)
* Laboratory studies demonstrating a link between televised violence and behavioral aggression (Geen & Thomas, 1986; Wood, Wong, & Chachere, 1991)
* the effects of an overrepresentation of young females and high status victims in the news (Mawby & Brown, 1984)

The Fear of Crime

The fear of being victimized by crime has been associated with various crime preventive actions and can create increased stress among affected individuals. Discussions can focus on the positive and negative aspects of victimization fear. Research evidence has suggested fear of crime differentiates among those who do or do not join community or neighborhood crime watches. Furthermore, specific crime reduction programs have been developed with varying rates of efficacy. Increased police presence has not been demonstrated to reduce fear (Bennett, 1991). However, programs designed to "empower" citizens have been demonstrated to increase defense skills and reduce victimization fear (Burke & Hayes, 1986).

Citizen Involvement in Police Matters

Community psychologists have developed programs to reduce the discrepancies among community residents and law enforcement officials concerning policing matters. Such programs aim to increase the participation of community residents in the determination, design, and delivery of crime prevention programs.

Secondary Prevention: Early Intervention Efforts

Following the initiation of criminal behavior the strategy of community psychologists shifts from preventive efforts to early detection and treatment. This section aims to familiarize students with the various intervention programs focusing primarily on juvenile delinquents. Specific emphasis is given to parental training, reducing recidivism in juvenile delinquents, and the provision of early services to crime victims.

Parental Training

Research evidence supports the efficacy of parental training as a secondary preventive intervention. Moreover, it has been argued that parental training offers the most promising technique for assisting juvenile offenders (Tolan, Cromwell, & Brasswell, 1986). Specifically, relative to no training controls, parent training groups have demonstrated lower offense rates, decreased institutionalization, and less subsequent police contact (Bank et al., 1991).

Reducing Recidivism in Juvenile Delinquents

The juvenile court system was developed to prevent youngsters from undergoing the stress of adult court procedures. However, given the more informal procedures, considerable variability exists concerning the professional decisions across similar cases. Some research suggests that service availability is the primary factor in treatment recommendations as opposed to the characteristics of the individual juvenile.

Among the different approaches to reduce the probability of recidivism the present chapter focuses on two; a multi-agency consultation program and New York's Mobile Mental Health Teams. Research on the efficacy of the former documented a recidivism rate that was one-fourth of the no-treatment cohorts. This program integrated educational, skills training, and familial involvement components. These programs provide examples of intermediate treatment provision which allow the juvenile to remain in the home environment with concomitant exposure to other environments.

Victim Assistance

While many secondary prevention programs target the offender, increasing concern about the victim has led to early victim assistance programs. Organizations such as The National Victims Resource Center provide educational materials and information on compensation programs. For this section students should be familiarized with the three types of early assistance provided to victims.

Crisis Intervention

Crisis intervention was developed as a set of procedures to help individuals recover from the effects of time-limited stress. Students can discuss the various examples of its use in current day events. Applications have included military disasters, natural disasters, and international terrorism.

Neighborhood Justice Centers

Neighborhood justice centers or community mediation centers provide an alternative to traditional court mediated conflict resolutions. Designed to handle cases from civil or criminal courts they assist the two parties in understanding and resolving their conflict in a mutually satisfactory fashion. Research suggests that about 85-90 percent of victims and defendants reported being satisfied with the outcome (Duffy, 1991). Discussion regarding the mechanisms of such success would be useful.

Problem-focused and emotion-focused coping

Such programs were developed to address the two immediate problems of victims, namely, the emotional distress of being victimized and decreasing the probability of revictimization. Students should be familiarized with various methods used to facilitate the two coping goals.

Tertiary Programs: Long Term Care

This section introduces the student to the various methods by which the criminal justice system and community psychology field address the problem of chronicity. Students are familiarized with the traditional areas of research. These included the efficacy of incarceration or imprisonment relative to alternative programs and the effect of pre-release programs during incarceration on recidivism rates.

Incarceration and its alternatives

Although, primarily the philosophy of the present day criminal justice system, the problems of incarceration including reduced social status, familial isolation, and lowered self-esteem have been well documented. Research evidence also suggests alternative forms of punishment such as **shock incarceration camps** or **boot camps** fall short of their specified goals. Students should be made aware of the various difficulties associated with conducting community research studies within this area and be familiarized with programs that have demonstrated some success.

Pre-release programs

Developed to ease the entry back into the community, pre-release programs have documented some success. Particularly, such programs have been used to facilitate the transition for forensic patients (incarcerated individuals with a mental disorder).

Intervention for victims

This section introduces the student to efforts directed at alleviating the emotional distress experienced by victims. Students should be familiarized with the effect of social support (both perceived and actual) as a buffering agent. Furthermore, the importance of matching the victim, the crime, and type of social support should be highlighted. Discussion should also be directed towards the "newer" victim-offender reconciliation programs.

Multiple Choice Questions

1. Community psychologists have been called upon to provide programs to assist in the _____ of criminal behavior.
    a. prediction   c. prevention
    b. retribution   * d. both a & c

2. _____ is an intentional act that violates the prescriptions or proscriptions of a law within the context of a particular society and historical era.
    a. A plea-bargain   * b. A crime
    c. An indictment   d. An arraignment

3. The field of psychology most likely to study the impact of legal phenomena on an individual is _____ .
    a. community psychology   b. clinical psychology
    * c. forensic psychology   d. criminal psychology

4. Often there is _____ correspondence between crimes that are committed and crimes that are reported.
    a. a high   * b. little
    c. no   d. frequent

5. Studies using cross-national comparisons should take into consideration a nation's_____.
    a. ethnic variations   b. racial relations
    c. cultural variety   d. subject sense of deprivation
    * e. all of the above

6. Cross-national studies of gun control do not allow for conclusions of causality because of their _____.
    * a. correlational nature   c. poor sampling techniques
    b. limited data base   d. both c and b

7. Studies have demonstrated that _____ is an important predictor of outcomes in both jury verdicts and sentencing decisions.
    a. violence   c. the type of crime
    * b. race   d. both c and b

8. Race has been demonstrated to play a role in _____.
   a. prosecutorial decisions in homicide cases
   b. sentencing decisions
   c. the prediction of outcomes in jury verdicts
   d. the probability of capital punishment
 * e. all the above

9. Almost _____ of those who are imprisoned are rearrested within three years of release.
   a. 10%   b. 35%   * c. 45%   d. 60%

10. In a classic psychological study, Zimbardo and his colleagues (1973) demonstrated:
   a. that even 'normal' volunteers are immune to the effects of the prison experience.
   b. that the prison experience is different for those who are incarcerated in authentic jails.
   c. that even 'normal' volunteers adhere to the proscribed roles of prisoner and guard.
   d. the prison experience can result in abusive behavior and negative emotional states.
 * e. both c & d.

11. The philosophical basis on which the present day legal system is based is that of _____.
 * a. retribution   c. rehabilitation
   b. punishment   d. retaliation

12. Presently, it is estimated that approximately _____ of all convicted offenders are being supervised in the community.
   a. 25%   b. 50%   * c. 75%   d. 85%

13. Innovative programs developed to address the increasing crowding and costs of imprisonment have included
   a. house arrest
   b. community service programs
   c. electronic monitoring
   d. both a & c
 * e. all the above

14. According to the "fear-victimization paradox" those living in a high crime environment should demonstrate a(n) _____ fear of victimization relative to those in a low crime environment.
   a. increased   c. equitable
 * b. decreased   d. none of the above

15. The sometimes supported inverse relationship between fear and actual victimization is known as the _____.
 * a. fear-victimization paradox
   b. PINS phenomena
   c. victimization phobia
   d. fear-crime paradox

16. Research supporting the fear-victimization paradox includes:
    a. young men, although most likely to be victimized, report being the least fearful.
    b. elderly women report being the most fearful yet are the least likely to be victimized.
    c. children, while being very fearful of crime, are the least likely to be crime victims.
    d. all of the above.
  * e. both a & b.

17. Explanations for the fear-victimization paradox have included:
    a. the perception of urban environments as dangerous
    b. the perception of the deterioration of social controls.
    c. a desensitization to the probability of crime.
  * d. all of the above
    e. both a & c

18. Taylor and Shumaker (1990) propose that crime may be conceptualized as a(n) _____.
    a. socialization process   * c. natural disaster
    b. cry for help   d. epidemic

19. A _____ aims to find global solutions to problems such as unemployment and other factors which may contribute to crime.
  * a. social problems orientation
    b. community psychology approach
    c. social-problem focus
    d. social-welfare orientation

20. Taylor and Shumaker (1990), propose that one global crime prevention program should be adapted to all neighborhoods.
    a. True   * b. False

21. A unique and important aspect of the criminal justice system is the increased responsibilities given to the victim in the legal process.
    a. True   * b. False

22. Research studies indicate that the treatment of victims within the legal system is _____ relative to other involved persons.
    a. equitable   c. more positive
  * b. more negative   d. none of the above

23. Research has indicated that juries tend to judge individuals as being _____ dangerous then they really are.
  * a. more
    b. juries have been shown to be fairly accurate
    c. less
    d. none of the above

24. Research suggests one of the better predictors of criminal behavior is _____.
  * a. previous delinquent behavior
    b. a familial history of crime
    c. an overly religious family
    d. all of the above
    e. both a and b

25. Which of the following family patterns has been associated with a lower probability of criminal behavior?
   a. low-conflict
   b. religiosity
   c. high cohesiveness
   d. all of the above
 * e. both a and c

26. Community psychology research suggests that interventions with "at-risk" youths should include:
   a. the youth's social network.
   b. an emphasis on one-to-one treatment approaches.
   c. the individual participating in the decision making process.
   d. all of the above
 * e. both a and c.

27. _____ study the effect of the environment on the behavior of individuals.
   a. Behavioral psychologists
 * b. Environmental psychologists
   c. Community psychologists
   d. Learning psychologists

28. _____ prevention programs are developed by community psychologists to alter criminal behavior prior its occurrence.
 * a. Primary   c. Secondary
   b. Tertiary   d. A priori

29. Environmental changes and neighborhood crime watches are examples of _____ crime prevention programs.
   a. secondary   c. tertiary
   b. active   * d. primary

30. _____ prevention programs are developed to intervene as early as possible following the initiation of criminal behavior.
   a. Primary   * c. Secondary
   b. Tertiary   d. Preliminary

31. _____, or the subjective experience of too many people for the amount of space, has been linked to negative affect and behavior.
 * a. Crowding   c. Enclosure
   b. Claustrophobia d. Isolation

32. Research has demonstrated features of our environments can and do influence crime rates.
 * a. True   b. False

33. Approximately _____ of children's cartoon's have been found to contain some violence.
   a. 50%   c. 75%
   b. 80%   * d. 90%

34. _____ studies have demonstrated a relationship between televised violence and behavioral aggression.
   a. Naturalistic   * c. Laboratory
   b. Field   d. Community
                         e. both a and c

35. Research suggests that continued exposure to violence can _____ us, leading to diminished emotional reactions.
     a. depress   c. buffer
   * b. desensitize   d. anger

36. A study by Mawby and Brown (1984) demonstrated that the media can distort the reality of violence. This was evidenced by the;
   a. overrepresentation of young females as victims.
   b. overrepresentation of high status victims.
   c. high prevalence of murder cases covered
   d. all of the above
 * e. both a & b.

37. Programs developed by community psychologists to reduce the fear of victimization have included;
 * a. neighborhood crime watches
   b. social support networks
   c. enforcement agencies
   d. community mediation centers
   e. all the above

38. Research indicates crime prevention groups;
   a. have no impact on property crimes
   b. reduce violent interpersonal crimes
 * c. have no impact on interpersonal crimes
   d. have no effect on crime in general

39. The reduction of the fear of crime has been related to programs which emphasize
   a. a strong police presence.
 * b. the empowerment of community members.
   c. strong familial involvement.
   d. positive role models.

40. Which of the following has been demonstrated to differentiate those who will join neighborhood crime watches from those who do not.
   a. family cohesiveness
   b. criminal history
   c. urbanicity
 * d. fear of crime

41. Secondary prevention programs focus on the _____ and _____ of criminal behavior.
   a. arraignment; indictment
 * b. detection; treatment
   c. detection; punishment
   d. treatment; retribution

42. _____ is considered by some to be among the most promising secondary prevention methods.
    a. Neighborhood crime watch
    b. The community police station program
*   c. Parental training
    d. Empowerment

43. Research examining the efficacy of parental training programs has demonstrated lowered rates of _____.
    a. offenses
    b. police contacts
    c. institutionalization
    d. both b & c
*   e. all of the above

44. The juvenile court system and the adult court system are similar with respect to the _____.
    a. procedural formality
    b. decision consistency
    c. service availability
    d. all of the above
*   e. none of the above

45. Research has demonstrated that one of the most important factors influencing treatment recommendations for juveniles is _____.
    a. family cohesion   c. prior convictions
*   b. service availability   d. peer support

46. Tolan, Perry, & Jones (1987) using a community based program for juveniles demonstrated a recidivism rate _____ that of no-treatment controls.
    a. one-third * b. one-fourth   c. half   d. equal to

47. The type of treatment based on the philosophy of allowing an individual to stay in their home environment while being introduced to a variety of other environments and programs.
    a. parole
    b. community-schooling
*   c. intermediate treatment
    d. primary prevention

48. Program(s) developed to assist individuals who have been victims of a crime include
    a. crisis intervention
    b. neighborhood justice centers
    c. problem/emotion focused coping
    d. both b & c
*   e. all of the above

49. _____, refers to programs developed to assist individuals recovering from temporary although extreme stress.
*   a. Crisis intervention
    b. Primary prevention
    c. Tertiary prevention
    d. Emotion-focused coping

50. Crisis intervention has been used to assist individuals in situations involving
    a. international terrorism
    b. military disasters
    c. sexual assaults
* d. all of the above

51. Research has demonstrated that the important ingredient(s) of a successful crisis intervention response includes;
    a. assessment
    b. emotional responding
    c. specific problem solving
    d. both a & c
* e. all of the above

52. Established in the local community, _____ offer an alternative to criminal and civil courts for the settling of disputes.
    a. neighborhood justice centers
    b. community-civil centers
    c. community mediation centers
* d. both a & c
    e. both b & c

53. Problems associated with incarceration have included:
    a. reduced social status
    b. lowered self-esteem
    c. decreased public assistance
* d. both a & b
    e. all of the above

54. Successful alternatives to incarceration, such as boot camps, have demonstrated a lower recidivism rate than the traditional confinement of criminals.
    a. True   * b. False

55. _____ programs were developed to ease the entry back into the community for incarcerated individuals.
* a. Pre-release
    b. Mediation
    c. Community transition
    d. Problem-focused

56. According to Kaniasty and Norris (1992), _____ social support demonstrated a positive buffering effect for victims of property and violent crimes.
    a. actual
* b. perceived
    c. familial
    d. peer

Identification of Terms

1. The process by which an individual is officially charged with a crime [Answer= Indictment]

2. An intentional act that violates the prescriptions or proscriptions of the criminal law under conditions in which no legal excuse applies and a state exists to enforce & codify the law. [Answer= crime]

3. The field of psychology which studies the impact of legal phenomena on individual behavior [Answer= forensic psychology]

4. The philosophy of incarceration and legal supervision which refers to the repayment for the particular crime committed. [Answer= retribution]

5. The phenomena by which the individuals who are most fearful of crime are the least likely to be victimized. [Answer= fear-victimization paradox]

6. The field of psychology which studies the effect of the environment on behavior. [Answer= environmental psychology]

7. A psychological intervention developed to help individuals recover from the effects of temporary or time-limited but extreme stress. [Answer=crisis intervention]

8. Centers that are established in the local community to handle cases from criminal and civil courts or other community agencies. [Answer= community mediation centers or neighborhood justice centers]

9. An alternative form of punishment run by corrections personal but resembles an intensive army training camp. [Answer= shock incarceration camps or boot camps]

10. Support received from significant others such as friends and family which can assist individuals' in coping with diverse emotions. [Answer= social support]

<u>Food For Thought</u>

I. "Plea bargaining" is one method by which the criminal justice system attempts to handle the large case load. First, discuss what is meant by plea-bargaining and present both the pros and cons of its use today.

[Answer Notes= Students should address the argument of the economic benefits and the possible negative effects on the poor and uneducated.]

II. Statistics have indicated that African-American males have the highest death rates from homicides. As such, various theories have been proposed to explain this phenomenon. Discuss the particular theories and associated supporting evidence addressing this issue.

[Answer Notes= students should discuss factors associated with income levels and Incardi's socio-economical theory.]

III. Some research studies have supported the fear-victimization paradox phenomenon. Describe what this phenomenon entails and the associated explanations for its occurrence.

IV. Both you and a friend are recently employed as community psychologists in the criminal justice system. Although, employed by the same organization you are both given different jobs. Specifically, your responsibilities include secondary prevention efforts and your friend has been put in charge of tertiary programs. Describe the differences between the two jobs and discuss the various types of programs for each.

[Answer Notes= students should demonstrate knowledge of the difference between secondary and tertiary intervention programs and provide examples of each such as parental training and incarceration alternatives.]

V. Victims sometimes are considered the "forgotten" players in the criminal justice system. Discuss what is meant by this and describe the type of services designed to address this perspective.

[Answer Notes= students should be aware of the limited role victims play in the traditional criminal justice system. Furthermore, discussion can focus on programmatic efforts at both the secondary and tertiary levels.]

Key Terms

Arraign
Boot camps
Capital punishment
Community mediation centers
Community police station program
Crime
Crisis intervention
Crowding
Enforcement agencies
Environmental psychology
Fear-victimization paradox
Forensic psychology
Incarceration
Indict
Intermediate treatment
Juvenile court system
Mediator/Mediation
Neighborhood crime watch
Neighborhood justice center
Parole
PINS (person in need of supervision)
Plea bargain
Pre-release program
Probation
Recidivate
Retribution
Shock incarceration camp
Social support
Total institutions
VORP (victim offender reconciliation program)

Recommended Films

Crime Control In Urban Environments Through Physical Planning And Design (Three 90 minute programs). This series features cases of urban projects that help prevent crime in housing areas, commercial districts, and institutional environments. PBS Adult Learning Satellite Service. PBS, 1320 Braddock Place Alexandria, VA 22314-1698.

The Peer Mediation Video (28 minutes). This program shows how to establish a successful peer mediation program with students in grades 6 through 12. Peer mediation is a nonadversarial process in which trained student mediators help fellow student solve their own problems. Research Press Catalog. Dept. N, P.O. Box 9177, Champaign, IL, 61826.

Black On Black Violence (26 minutes). This program includes discussions among inner-city experts and residents concerning the differential rates of violence against blacks today. Films for the Humanities & Sciences, P.O. Box 2053, Princeton, NJ 08543-2053.

Locking Up Women (48 minutes). This program looks at the philosophy of the changes and at the daily routine at a female-dominated prison. Films for the Humanities & Sciences, P.O. Box 2053, Princeton, NJ 08543-2053.

Street Gangs Of Los Angeles (44 minutes). This program looks at the thrills and dangers of life for black and Hispanic gang members. Furthermore, it highlights the occasionally successful efforts of parents to keep their children safe in these neighborhoods.

And Justice For All? This program examines the crisis in America's court system. This includes backlogged court s and the discrepancy in representation between the poor and economically advantaged. PBS Video Catalog. 1320 Braddock Place, Alexandria, Virginia, 22314-1698.

Crime And Punishments (60 minutes). Cruel and unusual punishment, from overcrowding in the prisons to the death penalty, is discussed by various criminal justice representatives. Corporation for Public Broadcasting, The Annenberg/CPB Project, 901 E Street, NW, Washington, DC 20004-2037.

Law, Order, And The Community (60 minutes). This program explores the drugs and law enforcement and highlights the frustrating battles both on the street and in the court room. Also includes an overview of the role of organized citizen groups acting without authority. PBS Video Catalog. 1320 Braddock Place, Alexandria, Virginia, 22314-1698.

CHAPTER 10

THE HEALTH CARE SYSTEM

Introduction

This chapter presents the Public Health Model and its application to three pertinent social issues: cigarette smoking, seat belt usage, and AIDS. The chapter begins by highlighting the strengths of America's current health care system. However, as the chapter illustrates, many citizens cannot afford health care costs. The Public Health Model emphasizes empowerment of individuals and prevention of disease. In order to combat cigarette smoking, automobile accidents, and AIDS, community psychologists must rely on societal level changes which utilize rewards, mass education, and skills training. Although the model stresses government intervention, experts disagree on how much intervention is appropriate.

Lecture and Notes

I. Background

The United States's medical community is one of the most technologically advanced in the world. For example, the state of California alone has more magnetic resonance imaging scanners than all of Canada. Americans also pride themselves on their ability to make choices about health care. However, the full picture is not perfect. Many Americans are uninsured and thus unable to receive adequate health care services. The question is how to address this problem. Some experts have advocated the Public Health model to tackle medical costs and health care in this country.

II. Public Health Model

The American Public Health Association was established in 1872 and included Margaret Sanger's pioneering work on the establishment of maternity clinics for low income women in New York City. Since its inception, the public health model has emphasized preventive medicine and the provision of early intervention services to community members.

Former U.S. Surgeon General Julian Richmond enhanced the model's credibility by outlining a set of goals which would improve the health of Americans within a 10-year period. These goals included a reduction in the number of cigarette smokers as well as a reduced infant mortality rate. Encouragingly, the infant mortality rate in the United States sharply declined until Presidents Reagan and Bush reduced pertinent social programs. Healthy People 2000 outlines another set of public health goals, which include reduced lead in drinking water and reduced infant mortality and morbidity rates.

The public health model has been somewhat successful. For example, cigarette smoking within the United States has decreased dramatically due to a strong social emphasis on prevention. The implementation of forceful media campaigns, stringent laws, and assertiveness skills training within schools have all contributed to reduced cigarette smoking.

Of course, the public health model emphasizes cultural sensitivity as well as a respect for gender differences. For example, research has shown that alcohol use/abuse increases among Hispanic-Americans with increased acculturation, although Hispanic-American females demonstrate greater alcohol use/abuse than their male counterparts. Research by Gilbert and Cervantes (1986) is cited.

Despite its efficacy, some critics reject the Public Health model. Most notably, critics argue that the model will impose on free choice and promote "socialized medicine." There is concern that government will punish individuals not conforming with governmental health standards, as is done in Canada and Singapore.

III. Tobacco Related Diseases: Preventable Deaths

Tobacco use has a number of pernicious health consequences, including increased risk for heart and blood problems, chronic bronchitis, emphysema, and lung cancer. Women who smoke during pregnancy are more likely to give birth to low weight infants and preterm babies (approximately 14% of all preterm births are attributable to smoking). Even environmental tobacco smoke (i.e., second hand smoke) is a recognized carcinogen, responsible for about 3,000 deaths per year in non-smoking individuals.

In response to these data, anti-smoking efforts have increased in recent years. For example, the National Cancer Institute (NCS) now funds 17 longitudinal smoking-reduction projects in 17 states. The NCS uses a tripartite model which emphasizes media, policy, and services/programs. Innovative and well-funded programs have also been initiated by California and Massachusetts and are described by the authors.

Smoking rates are disproportionately higher among African-Americans, blue collar workers, and the less educated. Furthermore, although the use of illicit drugs among adolescents has decreased during the past decade, smoking among adolescent females appears to be on the rise. This may be related the great advertising push by the tobacco industry, which has tripled the amount of money invested in advertising and promotions since 1975. Community psychologists advocate strong environmental manipulations (i.e., rewards and punishments) in order to combat efforts by the smoking industry. The authors provide an illustrative example of such community, discussing the joint work of psychologist Leonard Jason and policeman Bruce Talbot.

IV. Seat Belts: Roadwarriors

The lack of seat belt usage is a significant public health problem in this country. As the authors point out, more Americans die in auto crashes each year and a half than soldiers were killed in all ten years of the Vietnam War! To combat this trend, community psychologist have implemented innovative strategies to increase seat belt usage. Their effectiveness is supported by the data. For example, Berry and Geller (1991) used visual and auditory prompts to increase seat belt usage among drivers. Ludwig and Geller (1991) found that a personal commitment to use one's seat belt increased seat belt usage among some pizza deliverers. Finally, Nimmer and Geller (1988) found that carrying a pledge card and earning a five dollar incentive also increased seat belt usage among some drivers, and that many (but not all) continued to use their seat belts even after the monetary reinforcement was removed. Additional data provided by the authors indicate that stickers, bumper strips, and pizza dinners will increase seat belt usage among children.

V. AIDS: A Public Health Crisis

The human immunodeficient virus (HIV) is generally considered to responsible for the acquired immunodeficiency syndrome (AIDS), which has claimed more than 15 million lives to date. Estimates are that 20 million individuals in the world will be HIV positive by the year 1995. HIV is not the cause of AIDS, although it does open the door for "opportunistic infections" which lead to AIDS. Although initially identified in the homosexual community, AIDS is now common in the heterosexual community. There are many theories as to the origin of AIDS, including "green monkey" and biological warfare theories. Two experimental treatment drugs, AZT and ddI, are available to persons with AIDS. However, in order to receive these treatments, the individual must have more than 20 symptoms as defined by the Center of Disease Control and Prevention. Because of these constraints, illegal drugs are smuggled into the United States and sold to persons who are HIV positive or who have AIDS. Many people have died from these drugs, which led to a formal listing of all drug treatments for AIDS by American Foundation for AIDS Research.

Using the Public Health Model, community psychologists have emphasized attitudinal and behavioral changes to prevent the disease. Along these lines, students should know the "Health Belief Model," which emphasizes the interaction of perceived vulnerability, perceived severity of the disease, perceived barriers to health-protective action, and beliefs about self-efficacy to protect oneself from disease. Based on this model, prevention programs have been multifaceted and incorporated media programs, needle exchange, and safe sex outreach workshops. For example, Crawford and Jason (1990) used television media programs to successfully increase AIDS awareness and knowledge among children.

Students should be familiar with studies that have capitalized on "perceived social norms" to change behaviors. For example, Kelly et al. (1991) tested the effectiveness of community leaders trained in communication skills and safe sex practices. Community members exposed to these models reported increased knowledge about HIV and AIDS as well as safer sex practices than community members not exposed to the leader. Similar findings were replicated among Latino hustlers in New York City (Miller & Klotz, 1993). Finally, Watters et al. (1990) distributed vials of bleach to encourage drug users to clean their needles. Results indicated that a significant number of drug users cleaned their needles with the bleach and did not share needles during the preceding year. Increased condom usage was also reported.

Cognitive-behavioral interventions have also been used to increase condom usage. For example, Colson et al. (1993) have started a program called "Sex, Play, and Games" for homeless, mentally ill men. As discussed by the authors, this program used skills training, competition, and prizes to increase HIV/AIDS knowledge and safe sex practices.

Multiple Choice Questions

1. Which of the following statements is true?
   a. Due to a shortage in MRI scanners in California, Canada had to donate several of its extras to the citizens of California.
   b. The American Public Health Association was established in 1950.
   * c. Julian Richmond was the Surgeon General of the United States.
   d. President Reagan's social policies were consistent with the Public Health model.

2. Tobacco use ...
   a. does not include smokeless tobacco
   * b. includes smokeless tobacco
   c. is responsible for one of every ten deaths in the United States.
   d. has not been linked to oral cancer.

3. What percentage of babies are preterm due to smoking?
   * a. 14%
   b. 34%
   c. 64%
   d. 84%

4. What percentage of women continue to smoke during their pregnancies?
   a. 10%
   * b. 25%
   c. 40%
   d. 50%

5. Environmental tobacco smoke...
   a. has not yet been identified as a known carcinogen.
   b. has been associated with bronchitis and pneumonia in adults but not in children.
   * c. has been associated with bronchitis and pneumonia in infants and in children up to 18 months old.
   d. none of the above is correct.

6. The National Cancer Institutes's longitudinal studies on smoking emphasize a tripartite model which includes all of the following except...
   a. media services
   b. policy
   c. services and programs
   * d. all of the above

7. Cigarette smoking among _____ is on the rise.
   a. adolescent males
   * b. adolescent females
   c. adolescent males and females
   d. middle-aged women

8. Since 1979 the tobacco industry has ...
   a. reduced money spent on promotions and advertising.
   b. doubled money spent on promotions and advertising.
   * c. has tripled money spent on promotions and advertising.
   d. has quadrupled money spend on promotions and advertising.

9. The Health Belief Model ...
   a. emphasizes the role of perceived vulnerability to disease but not perceived severity of disease.
   b. emphasizes the role of perceived vulnerability to disease but not feeling of self-efficacy to protect oneself from disease.
   c. emphasizes the role of unconscious forces which drive unhealthy and destructive behaviors.
 * d. emphasizes both the perceived severity of the disease and perceived barriers to health-protective action.

10. Environmental tobacco smoke is classified as a _____ carcinogen.
 * a. Group A
   b. Group B
   c. Possible
   d. Potential

11. According to the text, which two states are engaging in the most comprehensive tobacco prevention and control programs in the United States?
   a. California and New York
   b. Massachusetts and New York
 * c. California and Massachusetts
   d. Colorado and Massachusetts

12. Research by DiFranza and colleagues indicates that ...
   a. "Joe Camel" was recognized as readily as "Mickey Mouse" by children.
   b. "Mickey Mouse" was more readily recognized than "Joe Camel" by children.
 * c. "Joe Camel" was more readily recognized than "Mickey Mouse" by children.
   d. "Joe Camel" was recognized more readily than "Smokey the Bear" by children.

13. There are _____ traffic deaths each day in the United States.
   a. 50
 * b. 125
   c. 300
   d. 500

14. More Americans die in traffic accidents every _____ than the total number of soldiers killed during all 10 years of the Vietnam war.
   a. year
 * b. year and a half
   c. three years
   d. ten years

15. In order to remind drivers to "buckle up," Berry and Geller (1991) designed a reminder system which relied upon...
 * a. visual and auditory cues
   b. visual and tactile cues
   c. auditory and tactile cues
   d. Auditory and olfactory cues

16. Nimmer and Geller (1988) tried to increase seat belt usage among drivers by having them sign and display a pledge card, and allowing them to earn a $5.00 money incentive. The authors discovered that...
   a. the monetary incentive discouraged seat belt usage.
   * b. seat belt usage decreased somewhat after removal of the monetary incentive from the program.
   c. the program became totally ineffective after the monetary incentive was removed.
   d. drivers refused to display the card in their vehicles.

17. Research attempting to increase safety belt usage among children ...
   a. has been consistently ineffective at increasing safety usage among this age group.
   b. has increased safety belt usage by using stickers and bumper strips, but not food, as rewards.
   c. has increased safety belt usage by using food, but not stickers or bumper strips, as rewards.
   * d. has increased safety belt usage by using food, stickers, and bumper strips as rewards.

18. Citizens of _____ showed greater public opposition than citizens of _____ to imposed seat belt laws in these two geographic areas.
   * a. Yugoslavia; Illinois
   b. Illinois; Yugoslavia
   c. Russia; Illinois
   d. none of the above is correct

19. There is a small group of scientists which argues that HIV is not responsible for AIDS. According to these authors, this hypothesis...
   a. is starting to become the leading hypothesis held by most researchers.
   * b. is generally ignored by the mainstream scientific community.
   c. is receiving more serious attention in recent years by the mainstream scientific community.
   d. is shared by university professors but not by the mainstream medical community.

20. Which of the following was advocated for by Margaret Sanger?
   a. greater funding for AIDS research
   b. reduced cigarette smoking
   c. reduced amounts of led in drinking water
   * d. more maternity clinics for low income women

21. Dr. Julian Richmond proposed a series of goals to improve American health ...
   a. within a 1 year period
   b. within a 5 year period
   * c. within a 10 year period
   d. within a 15 year period

22. Which of the following statements is true?
    a. President Bush's policies were consistent with the public health model.
    b. The infant mortality rate had risen dramatically until the Reagan/Bush administrations--at which point the rate began to decline.
    c. Virtually all public health goals outlined by Dr. Julian Richmond have been successfully attained.
  * d. The "public health model" is consistent with the field of community psychology.

23. Attempts to reduce cigarette smoking using the public health model have included...
    a. mass media efforts
    b. school-based programs
    c. cognitive-behavioral skills training
  * d. all of the above are true

24. Alcohol use/abuse among Hispanic Americans...
  * a. is more common among females than males.
    b. decreases with acculturation
    c. is more common among males than females
    d. is affected by neither acculturation nor gender

25. Which of the following statements is true?
    a. third world countries have generally been immune from HIV and AIDS.
    b. AIDS was first noticed in the United States predominately among intravenous drug users.
    c. most scientists are in agreement as to the origin of HIV and AIDS.
  * d. most scientists are unsure as to the origins of HIV and AIDS.

26. In order to receive AZT, an individual...
    a. must be identified with AIDS and not just have HIV.
  * b. must have at least 20 symptoms as defined by the Centers of Disease Control and Prevention.
    c. must not take any other medication.
    d. all of the above are true.

27. Which of the following statements is true?
    a. AIDS is caused by the HIV virus
    b. The prevalence of AIDS among children is expected to significantly decline before the year 2000.
  * c. A small group of scientists believes that the HIV virus is not responsible for AIDS.
    d. All of the above are true.

28. _____ opens the door for _____ which leads to _____.
    a. AIDS; opportunistic infections; HIV
  * b. HIV; opportunistic infections; AIDS
    c. opportunistic infections; HIV; AIDS
    d. opportunistic infections; AIDS; HIV

29. "ARC" stands for...
    a. AIDS Related Condition
    b. AIDS Relegated Complex
  * c. AIDS Related Complex
    d. AIDS Rearing Condition

30. Which of the following is a cure for AIDS?
    a. AZT
    b. ddI
    c. both a & b
  * d. neither a nor b

31. Watters et al. (1990) distributed bleach-filled vials along with instructions for safe sex to intravenous drug users (IVDU's). The authors found that...
    a. IVDU's used the bleach to clean their needles, but did not increase condom usage.
    b. IVDU's discontinued all safe sex practices.
  * c. IVDU's used the bleach to clean their needles and also increased condom usage.
    d. IVDU's increased condom usage, but did not use the bleach to clean their needles.

32. Kelly et al. (1991) found that _____ predicted condom usage by gay and bisexual men.
  * a. peer pressure
    b. educational literature
    c. monetary incentives
    d. fear induction

33. According to the Health Beliefs Model, readiness to perform health-related behaviors is a function of all of the following except...
    a. perceived vulnerability
    b. perceived severity of disease
  * c. religion
    d. all of the above

34. The _____ states that the performance of health-related behaviors is a function of perceived vulnerability, perceived severity of disease, perceived barriers to health-protective action, and feelings of self-efficacy.
    a. Social Norms Model
  * b. Health Belief Model
    c. Health Norms Model
    d. Public Health Model

35. Which of the following statements is true regarding multifaceted programs designed to promote AIDS prevention?
    a. Because these programs are so large, it is easy to determine which elements of the program "caused" it to succeed or fail.
    b. Programs have been developed for gay men in large urban areas, but not intravenous drug users.
    c. Programs have been developed for intravenous drug users, but not gay men.
  * d. Programs often include mass media educational programs.

36. High school students may be more likely to purchase and use condoms if their peers as doing so. This point exemplifies the value of ...
  * a. perceived social norms
    b. multifaceted education programs
    c. perceived self-efficacy
    d. none of the above

37. Miller and Klotz (1991) implemented an HIV prevention program among Latino hustlers in New York City. Results indicated that their program had direct effects on ...
    a. HIV risk knowledge
    b. HIV risk behavior
    c. HIV risk norms
* d. all of the above

38. The intervention program "Sex, Play, and Games" was developed for which of the following groups?
    a. Latino hustlers
    b. homosexual males
* c. homeless and mentally ill men
    d. intravenous drug users

39. Which of the following statements about the intervention program called "Sex, Play, and Games" is true?
    a. participants reported greater HIV and AIDS knowledge, but no change in risky sexual behavior.
    b. participants reduced sexually risky behavior, although their knowledge of HIV and AIDS did not increase.
* c. participants competed against one another with the "winner" receiving a prize.
    d. the intervention program provided information but no skills training to participants.

40. Which of the following statements best reflects the dilemma facing community psychologists trying to implement the Public Health Model?
    a. Should government intervene in the implementation of community programs?
* b. How much should government intervene in the implementation of community programs?
    c. When should government intervene in the implementation of community programs?
    d. Should community psychologists and lawmakers work together to tackle social problems?

Identification of Terms

1. Births which occur at or before the 37th week of gestation.
    (Answer= Preterm birth).

2. Exposure to another individual's tobacco smoke.
    (Answer= Environmental tobacco smoke).

3. Unwritten social rules which people are expected to follow. (Answer= Perceived social norms).

4. Organization which funds 17 longitudinal studies in 17 states in order to investigate tobacco use. (Answer= National Cancer Institute).

5. Two countries which have socialized medicine. (Answer= Canada and Singapore).

6. Model of behavior which emphasizes the interaction of perceived vulnerability, disease severity, barriers to action, and self-efficacy. (Answer= Health Belief Model).

7. Illness/disease which leads to full blown AIDS. (Answer= Opportunistic infection).

8. Drug treatment for AIDS. (Answer= AZT or ddI).

9. Model which emphasizes preventive medicine and is stressed by community psychologists. (Answer= Public Health Model).

10. Name of virus which allows for AIDS to develop. (Answer= Human Immunodeficiency Virus).

Food for Thought

I. Some smokers argue that tobacco smoke has no effect on anybody except themselves (the smokers) and, therefore, laws to eliminate cigarette smoking are unfair. Is this true? Does tobacco smoke do harm to other individuals? Answer this question using data discussed in the chapter.

II. Why do some authorities dislike the Public Health Model approach to health care? What are their objections? How do advocates of the Public Health Model respond to these concerns?

[Answer notes: Objection to Public Health Model deal with high values many Americans place on choice for medical services. Many fear socialized medicine. Advocates focus on the effectiveness of government interventions in areas of tobacco smoke and seat belt usage.]

III. Imagine that you teach community psychology to a class of undergraduates. One of your students argues that the Public Health Model is very limited because it only works for "mentally healthy adults." How would you explain to your student that (s)he is wrong! Discuss studies and data which do not support this argument. What are some "nontraditional" samples that have been studied? Have interventions with these groups been effective?

[Answer notes: Discussion should focus on research conducted with mentally ill men, prostitutes, hustlers, and children reviewed in the chapter.]

IV. What is the difference between "focused" and "multifaceted" treatment interventions? Give examples of each from the seat belt, tobacco, and/or AIDS literature.

V. As director of public health in your dormitory, you are concerned about the prevalence of HIV and AIDS among your residents. Based on the research on perceived social norms discussed in the chapter, develop a program to promote condom use among your dormitory residents. Justify each component of your program.

Key Terms

Acquired immunodeficiency syndrome

Diffusion model
Empower(ment)
Environmental tobacco smoke
Family planning
Health Belief Model
Health promotion
Human immunodeficiency virus
Intervention
Intravenous drug users
Low weight infants
National Cancer Institute
Perceived social norms
Preterm births
Preventive medicine
Public health model
Second hand smoke
Smoking
Social norms
Socialized medicine
Tobacco use
Treatment

Recommended Films

<u>AIDS Education</u> (28 minutes). This program examines innovative AIDS education programs in a San Francisco first grade class and a New Hampshire high school. Former Surgeon General C. Everett Koop and others are interviewed. Films For The Humanities & Sciences, Inc. P.O. Box 2053, Princeton, N.J. 08543-2053.

<u>AIDS Fighters</u> (30 minutes). This show features stories about teens who are on the front line in the fight against AIDS. PBS Video, 1320 Braddock Place, Alexandria, VA 22314-1698. Fax: 703-739-5269.

<u>AIDS: The Changed Face of America</u> (52 minutes). This special two-part Phil Donahue program examines how AIDS has changed a variety of practices in American culture, including dating practices, homophobia, social and job discrimination, and health care practices. Films For The Humanities & Sciences, Inc. P.O. Box 2053, Princeton, N.J. 08543-2053.

<u>AIDS, The Family, and The Community</u> (26 minutes). This program shows how AIDS is transmitted, how many cases of infection are the result of sexually active teens' believing that it can't happen to them, the importance of community support for persons with AIDS, and how this epidemic affects all of us. Films For The Humanities & Sciences, Inc. P.O. Box 2053, Princeton, N.J. 08543-2053.

<u>An Ounce of Prevention</u> (60 minutes). This film depicts several social programs that are attempting to eliminate risk factors for psychological disorders. These risk factors include social isolation, inadequate parenting skills, and old age. The Annenberg/CPB Project. 901 E. Street, NW., Washington, DC 20004-2037.

<u>Other Faces of AIDS</u> (60 minutes). This program focuses on the rapid spread of AIDS in minority communities. Included are interviews with C. Everett Koop, Jessie Jackson, and other educators and researchers involved with

these issues. PBS Video, 1320 Braddock Place, Alexandria, VA 22314-1698. Fax: 703-739-5269.

<u>Pandemic</u> (60 minutes). Illustrates innovative programs for preventing AIDS among high risk populations in the community. Examples include programs for homeless persons in Miami, educational approaches for Bangkok's thriving sex industry, and community services in Australia. PBS Video, 1320 Braddock Place, Alexandria, VA 22314-1698. Fax: 703-739-5269.

CHAPTER 11

COMMUNITY ORGANIZATIONAL PSYCHOLOGY

Introduction

This chapter demonstrates the similarities between organizational and community psychology. In particular, the chapter illustrates how the field of organizational development attempts to improve business productivity while enhancing individual workers. The chapter begins by reviewing common workplace problems, such as workaholism, burnout, and poor environmental work conditions. Traditional management strategies (e.g., compensation packages, rules and regulations, discipline) are contrasted against alternative strategies which are consistent with the community model (e.g., QWL programs, team building, quality circles, job expansion, MBO, realistic job preview). The authors review the effectiveness of some newer programs and conclude that organizations should pay greater attention to the needs of individual workers.

Lecture and Notes

I. Organizational & Community Psychology

Despite being two distinct fields of psychology, organizational and community psychology do share some commonalities:

a) Both develop paradigms or models as well as constructs and measurement techniques which go beyond the level of the individual. That is, both deal with groups of individuals. For example, organizational psychologists have advanced the notion of "Organizational Development" (OD)--a set of social science techniques designed to improve organizational functioning and enhance individuals within the organization.

"Survey Guided Feedback" is one type of OD technique. Using this procedure, periodic surveys are conducted throughout the organization to assess employee/client attitudes and feelings. Results are shared with all levels of the organization.

b) Both community and organizational psychologists also understand that communities have a dynamic, transactional relationships which vary over time.

c) Both community and organizational psychologists have a multilevel (or, holistic) approach to the organization. That is, both recognize the interplay between the various levels within the organization. However, despite these claims, McClure et al. (1980) found that less than ten percent of the articles published in the American Journal of Community Psychology emphasized a system or organizational focus.

d) Both community and organizational psychologists argue that work has consequences for psychological well-being. That is, our work effects how we feel about ourselves.

Despite these similarities, community and organizational psychology do have differences:

a) Organizational psychology fundamentally aims to increase monetary profits while deemphasizing personal growth. Empowering individuals is not necessarily the goal. On the other hand, as this book has argued, community psychologists strive for empowerment of individuals in addition to organizational functioning.

However, managers within organizations are now paying more attention to empowerment of individual workers. For example, "Quality of Work Life" programs are becoming more common in the workplace.

"Quality Circles" are one type of quality of worklife program. Quality circles are small groups of volunteer employees who regularly meet to identify and solve organizational problems.

II. Everyday Problems in Today's Community Organizations

Stress

We can define stress as "a call for action when one's capabilities are perceived as falling short of the needed personal resources" (Sarason, 1980). Thus, stress can be produced by both positive and negative life events. Even minor, everyday hassles contribute to stress. Organizational life can produce stress in a variety of ways. Interpersonal conflict, noxious environmental conditions, and poor rule structures are just a few examples.

Burnout

We can define burnout as "a feeling of overall exhaustion which is the result of too much pressure and not enough sources of satisfaction" (Moss, 1981). Individuals with burnout blindly follow job rule and procedures while their job performance deteriorates.

Burnout has three components:
--The feeling of being drained or exhausted.
--Depersonalization.
--A sense of low personal accomplishment or that one's efforts are futile.

Some additional facts about burnout:
--It is most likely to occur among organizational members who are initially eager, motivated, and idealistic about their jobs (Van Fleet, 1991).
--Burnout is more likely to occur among staff when they focus excessively on client progress rather than their own personal growth and development. Thus, in order to combat burnout, staff members should receive organizational feedback on their growth and development and not just feedback from clients (Eisenstat & Felner, 1984).

Workaholism

Type A personalities have a chronic state of urgency, competitiveness, and impatience. They are more likely to be workaholics than are "Type B" personalities, who are more relaxed and flexible. Interestingly, Type A personalities are more likely to live in industrialized and densely populated cities rather than small rural communities (Rosenman & Chesney, 1982). The higher prevalence of heart attack among Type A personalities is due to their chronic hostility and cynicism.

Organizational Structure

Organizational structure consists of the beliefs, attitudes, values, and expectations shared by organizational members (Schein, 1985, 1990). These structures persist over time and generally set the tone for an organizations. They also determine power distribution, that is, who decides how organizational funds will be spent. For example, the organizational structure might dictate that only executives decide employee work schedules and that policies such as flexitime (see below) are not permitted. On the other hand, organizations which value human input and growth might encourage employee input into decision making.

Along these lines, the authors distinguish between "open" and "repressive" cultures within organizations. Open organizations value human dignity and growth and encourage a sense of community with the organization. Repressive cultures discourage organizational cohesion. Instead, cynicism and hostility are promoted, leading to an unpleasant work environment. Interestingly, research by Petty and McCarthy (1991) suggests gender differences in what constitutes a "sense of community." For male workers, a sense of community comes from strong peer cohesion. For female workers, perceptions of supervisor support were more important.

Environmental conditions

A variety of environmental factors can impede performance. As indicated in the chapter, temperature and humidity impede performance. Loud noises damage hearing. The size of the organization can also be detrimental. Research by Hellman et al. (1985) demonstrated greater anxiety, worse psychosocial job appraisals, and greater psychological distance from the organization within larger organizations.

Poor Human Resource Management

To address organizational problems, organizations call upon "human resource management" (HRM) services. HRM (or, personnel administration) ideally functions as a problem solving agent--recruiting, training, and appraising staff in order to facilitate the growth of the organization and personnel. However, HRM might not meet the needs of all personnel. Consequently, some might feel disenfranchised and disempowered from the organization.

III. Traditional Techniques for Managing Organizations

Organizations have traditionally relied upon a restricted menu of techniques for handing personnel problems. The chapter reviews each of these techniques, along with their limitations.

Compensatory packages

Many organizations believe that increased pay leads to greater job satisfaction. However, the data do not necessarily support this view. Personnel rarely rate salary as the most essential element to their job satisfaction (Schultz & Schultz, 1990). Even when salaries are raised, they only partially increase job satisfaction (Sarata, 1984).

Rules and regulations

Although many organizations have strict rules which regulate behavior, employees prefer to make their own rules. They often dislike authoritarian command and prefer to participate in decision making. This even holds true for dormitory residents. Triplett et al. (1988) found greater compliance to dormitory rules when they were able to participate in making the rules than when they had no input. Furthermore, classic research conducted at the Western Electric Plant in Hawthorne demonstrated that employees <u>purposely</u> worked below the regulated standard because they feared that the standard would otherwise be raised! Thus, overly rigid rules do not appear to enhance a sense of community within organizations.

Discipline

Many employees get disciplined at work. Disciplinary action is most frequently implemented for attendance problems (60% of terminations), followed by performance problems (17%), drug or alcohol use (9%), and other reasons (14%). Nonetheless, employee termination is costly to the individual and the organization--that is, it has a "systems impact." For example, organizations which dismiss workers need to invest time in recruiting and training new employees.

IV. Overview of Organizational Change

Reasons for change

Internal and external pressures are major sources of change. Internal pressures stem from within the organization (e.g, staff, supervisors, clients). External pressures stem from outside the organization (e.g., government, public opinion, media).

Issues related to change

There are various factors which impede efforts at organizational change. First, many individual employees fear any change and thus become resistant. Second, organizations are interdependent. Thus, even small changes have large impacts. Third, any attempt at intervention must occur within the organizational paradigm (structure). For example, even self-help groups vary in structure. Some are "dependent on external funds" while others rely on "internal experiential authority." Thus, successful efforts at change might be dependent on the appropriate self-help group for the appropriate organizational structure.

V. Changing the Whole Organization

The chapter discusses two types of whole organization change: reorganization and quality of life programs.

Reorganization

Reorganization refers to broader structural changes which occur, for example, in job tasks, interpersonal relationships, and reward systems. Reorganizations can take various forms. For example, organizational size can be decreased or links to enabling systems can be established. These changes are structural in nature.

Quality of life programs (QWL)

QWL programs strive towards "participatory decision making" within organizations. That is, input on programs comes from various personnel and clients. Such strategies have been demonstrated to improve organizational productivity and job satisfaction.

Some critics claim that large organizations lack sensitivity and humanitarian values. To combat this, some organizations have implemented "sensitivity (T-group) training," which incorporates lectures and experiential exercises to enhance the interpersonal relations and communications among personnel. Available literature suggests that QWL programs are effective at promoting self-generated change. Students should be aware of a study by Hamilton and colleagues (1985) which demonstrated that adolescents encouraged to work more independently, to increase work complexity, and to be work more responsibly showed significant gains in moral and social reasoning. Still, QWL programs do have disadvantages. For example, participants might encounter added bureaucracy and less free time.

VI. Group change within the organization

Groups play an instrumental role in organizational change. Group characteristics such as role differentiation, group organization, and perceptions of leaders all contribute to group members' well-being and their liking for the group. These variables were studied within the context of self-help groups (Maton, 1988) and discussed in the chapter.

There are various methods for group change within organizations. Team building and quality circles are two such methods:

a) Team building is an ongoing group method with two goals: (1) to analyze tasks, member relations, and interpersonal processes, and (2) to accomplish goals. Team building is the most popular OD method and has been demonstrated to be effective by meta-analytic studies. This technique has been used in a variety of contexts (e.g., prisons, methadone maintenance clinics, schools) and with a variety of subjects (e.g., nurses, physicians).

b) Quality circles involve small groups of volunteers who meet regularly to identify and solve problems related to organizational conditions. They have been used with teachers, college students, and government employees, although they are less popular than team building methods.

VII. Helping Individuals Change

Stress and Burnout

Although meditation and relaxation have been the traditional methods for helping personnel to cope with stress, community psychologists have developed alternative methods which strive toward greater organizational change. These methods are reviewed by the authors.

a) Increasing social support is one important method for change. Co-workers can model coping strategies, give practical advice, and show empathy. Students should be aware of the various studies demonstrating the efficacy of social support across different populations (e.g., social workers, the unemployed, and corrections officers). However, some research suggests that social support can actually worsen a situation (Grossi & Berg, 1991).

b) Constructive feedback provides personnel with information on their job performance. "Performance appraisals" are formal reviews of an employee's job performance. Feedback of this nature can reduce job stress and burnout. This has been demonstrated among prison correction officers (Digman et al., 1986) and human service workers (Eisenstat & Felner, 1984).

c) Mass education programs, such as television programs on stress management, can also be helpful. The authors describe a study by Jason and colleagues (1989), whose television series on stress and coping had positive effects on viewer adjustment and well-being. These effects were most pronounced among the most distressed viewers.

Other Personal Problems

a) Smoking. Although smoke cessation programs exist, recidivism is a major barrier to long-term change. Social support may be an essential variable for preventing relapse. At least one study found that the availability of group meetings was the best predictor of 12-month smoking abstinence (Jason et al., 1989).

b) Family dysfunction and employment. Many families today have two working parents and this raises problems for child care. Fortunately, there are solutions to this problem:

"Work schedule adaptations" allow personnel to select where and when they will work. The authors discuss "flexitime," one type of work schedule adaptation. Flexitime allows personnel to select the total number of hours worked, the length of the work week, or other variations, although there are core hours during which personnel must be at the organization.

"Compressed workweeks" generally allow personnel to work four ten-hour work days, with either Monday or Friday off. "Home work," another alternative discussed in the chapter, allows individuals to work at home for all or a portion of the work. Home computers typically link the home office to the organizational headquarters.

"Employee Assistance Programs" (EAP's) are in-house programs designed to help employees with personal problems. The number of EAP's has grown rapidly in the past two decades. EAP's are often tied to "wellness programs." Wellness programs promote healthy behaviors in order to prevent subsequent illness and often focus of diet, weight loss, and lifestyle modification.

VIII. Changing Jobs

Alternative strategies have recently been developed for promoting well-being at the workplace. Students should be familiar with these innovative strategies.

Job Expansion

There are at least two types of job expansion: job enlargement and job enrichment. Job enlargement means adding more work to the job, although the new work requires the same level of job skill. On the other hand, job enrichment means adding higher level responsibilities to one's job. That is, new challenges are added.

As reviewed in the chapter, task interest is important aspect of job satisfaction. For example, workers are more likely to stay at stressful jobs as long the job responsibilities are interesting (Zautra et al., 1986). Job expansion also led to greater feelings of accomplishment and greater job satisfaction among corrections officers (Linquist & Whitehead, 1986).

Management by Objective (MBO)

MBO requires staff and supervisors to jointly discuss the tasks at hand and to determine how they will be accomplished. Goals are set together and joint evaluations are performed. The authors describe this process as a participative negotiation, which distinguishes it from traditional forms of management. Several studies are cited which illustrate the efficacy of MBO's within municipal governments, hospitals, the Equal Opportunity Commission, colleges, and police forces.

Realistic Job Previews (RJP)

RJP's provide job applicants with accurate descriptions of the job before they take it. That is, the strengths and limitations are openly discussed in order to prevent unrealistic and overly idealistic expectations. Overly idealistic expectation can lead to job burnout. Interestingly, the available data indicate no adverse effects to this type of candor (Shinn & Perkins, in press).

IX. Does OD Work?

This chapter has presented a variety of traditional and nontraditional methods for promoting organizational growth and individual development. In terms of OD effectiveness, the students should be aware of a major review article by Porras and colleagues (in press) which reviewed almost 50 OD studies between 1975 and 1986. The results are somewhat encouraging. Overall, OD is beneficial. However, it is more beneficial to the organization than to the individual. Furthermore, better results are obtained when more than one OD strategy is implemented. Thus, single effort strategies may not be extremely effective, especially in terms of promoting the development of the individual worker.

Multiple Choice Questions

1. _____ examines organizations from the perspective of the individual, whereas _____ examines organizations from a systems perspective.
    a. Organizational behavior; an EAP
    b. The quality circle; organizational behavior
  * c. Organizational psychology; organizational behavior
    d. The MBO; the EAP

2. Chavis & Florin (1990) found that survey guided feedback reduced inactivity in community organizations by ...
   a. 25%
 * b. 50%
   c. 75%
   d. 90%

3. Survey guided feedback ...
   a. is typically provided only to employees.
 * b. is provided in order to develop specific procedures for correcting organizational problems.
   c. is only provided to managers, who then decide whether or not to share it with the employees.
   d. all of the above are true.

4. Burnout consists of all of the following except...
   a. feelings of exhaustion
   b. insensitivity to others
 * c. breaking company rules
   d. none of the above

5. Burnout is less likely to occur if...
   a. new employees have excessively high job expectations.
   b. employers do not provide regular feedback to staff.
 * c. clients provide regular feedback to workers.
   d. the job is somewhat stressful.

6. Which of the following statements is true?
 * a. Chronic cynicism puts Type A personalities at risk for heart attack.
   b. Type A personalities are more likely to live in rural communities than in industrialized cities.
   c. Type B personalities experience a chronic sense of urgency.
   d. Type A personalities work at a maximum capacity only when they have strict deadlines.

7. Organizations can be described as which of the following?
   a. stable over time
 * b. fragmented
   c. holistic
   d. None of the above

8. McClure et al.'s (1980) study on the articles published in the American Journal of Community Psychology found that...
 * a. less than 10% focused on systems/organizational issues.
   b. only 25% focused on systems/organizational issues.
   c. approximately 50% focused on systems/organizational issues.
   d. over 80% focused on systems/organizational issues.

9. _____ consists of the beliefs, attitudes, values, and expectations shared by most members of the organization.
 * a. Organizational culture
   b. Organizational development
   c. The quality of worklife
   d. The quality circle

10. Organizational culture influences which of the following?
    a. organizational structure
    b. power distribution within the organization
    c. ideology of the organization
  * d. all of the above

11. Joe works in an organization which encourages his growth as a service provider by paying for his trips to professional conferences. This work culture might be described as being...
    a. repressed
  * b. open
    c. terminating
    d. all of the above

12. John and Susan are new managers at a local business. According to research by Pretty and McCarthy (1991) on organizational "sense of community"...
    a. John's sense of community is best predicted by his relationship with his boss.
    b. Susan's sense of community is best predicted by the cohesion she has with her peers.
  * c. John's sense of community is best predicted by the cohesion he has with his peers.
    d. Quality circles should be implemented immediately.

13. Which of the following environmental factors influences job performance?
    a. humidity
    b. room temperature
    c. excessive noise
  * d. all of the above

14. Hellman et al. (1985) surveyed anxiety among members of a residential mental health treatment program. Her data indicate that anxiety was...
  * a. associated with larger size programs.
    b. associated with smaller size programs.
    c. associated with programs promoting isolation.
    d. not related to the size of the program.

15. Compensation packages (e.g., offering employees a raise to stay at their jobs)...
    a. are rarely offered because they are too costly.
  * b. partially increase job satisfaction.
    c. typically decrease job satisfaction.
    d. none of the above are true.

16. Imagine that you trained a team of workers to manufacture pencils for classroom notes. You set a standard for them to produce 100 pencils per hour. According to the classic "wiring room" study conducted in Hawthorne, Illinois, you would expect...
  * a. workers to produce pencils at a rate below the standard.
    b. workers to produce pencils at a rate above the standard.
    c. workers to believe that your standard is permanently fixed and will not change so they work "at standard."
    d. workers to want even higher work standards.

17. Triplet et al. (1988) found greater compliance to dormitory rules among college undergraduates when...
    a. those rules were established by an authority.
    b. direct penalties were implemented for rule violation.
  * c. students participated in making the rules.
    d. rules were perceived as rigid and permanent.

18. Data indicate that employees are most frequently fired because of ...
  * a. attendance problems
    b. drug use
    c. inadequate job performance
    d. theft

19. Most traditional methods for regulating job behavior...
    a. are consistent with the model of community psychology.
    b. aim for organizational-level change rather than individual-level change.
    c. encourage individual participation in rule setting.
  * d. emphasize treatment rather than prevention.

20. Which of the following is an example of internal pressure to fire a baseball manager?
    a. Fans believe that he is incompetent.
    b. The media criticize him after every baseball game.
  * c. Team players have secretly voted that they want him to be fired.
    d. His parents think that he should be a doctor.

21. Research by Schubert & Borkman (1991) suggests that...
    a) all self-help groups generally follow the same model.
    b) there is little evidence for the concept of "organizational paradigms."
    c) there are three different types of self-help groups.
  * d) there are five different types of self-help groups.

22. According to the text's authors, organizational change should start with...
    a) the formation of quality circles.
  * b) action research.
    c) the formation of umbrella organizations.
    d) none of the above.

23. Changes within organizations can occur at which of the following levels?
    a) individual level
    b) group level
    c) organizational
  * d) All of the above

24. Which of the following interventions would community psychologists recommend in order to improve interpersonal relations and enhance openness among coworkers?
    a) enabling systems
  * b) T-groups
    c) performance appraisals
    d) compressed workweeks

25. Research by Hamilton et al. (1985) suggests that QWL programs...
   a) have little impact on adolescents' moral reasoning.
 * b) improve adolescents' moral reasoning.
   c) are too sophisticated to be used with adolescents.
   d) are less effective than discipline for improving adolescents' moral reasoning.

26. Harold is in charge of team building for the department of psychology. Specifically, he wants his department to strive towards more journal publications next year. As a team builder, Harold is interested in which of the following?
   a) How many more journal articles the department should strive towards (that is, the goal).
   b) How the department will obtain the goal of more publications (that is, the process).
   c) Relationships among fellow faculty members.
 * d) All of the above.

27. Which of the following statements is supported by the data?
   a) There have been very few studies to date on the effectiveness of team building. Thus, it's effectiveness if unknown.
 * b) Team building is quite effective.
   c) Team building is only effective for managers.
   d) Team building is not effective.

28. Team development has been used with which of the following samples?
   a) teachers.
   b) staff at psychiatric prisons.
   c) nurses.
 * d) all of the above.

29. Qualities circles...
   a) are used more extensively in community agencies than team building.
   b) require a small group of volunteer employees to meet only once in order to identify workers' organizational concerns.
 * c) have been used with teachers, college students, and government employees.
   d) all of the above are correct.

30. Olson (1991) found that social support encourages teachers...
 * a) to be more autonomous in their decisions.
   b) to be more dependent on others in their decisions.
   c) to avoid decision making.
   d) to make decisions more frequently for other teachers.

31. Research by Hirsch and David (1983) and McIntosh (1991) found that social support from fellow nurses...
    a) helped nurses to reduce their general stress level, although they reported no improvement in their ability to cope with patient death.
    b) helped nurses to cope better with patient death, although their general stress level did not change.
  * c) helped nurses to reduce their general stress level and cope better with patient deaths.
    d) led to less absenteeism and less sick leave from work.

32. Performance appraisals to employees about their work...
    a) are typically informal.
  * b) are typically formal.
    c) are most effective when given infrequently to workers.
    d) do not provide feedback to workers.

33. Research by Jason et al. (1989) demonstrated that TV programs designed to improve coping skills and stress management...
    a) had little beneficial effect on viewers.
    b) was only beneficial for the "healthier" viewers and not for the more "distressed" viewers.
  * c) led to improved viewer adjustment and well-being, especially among the most "distressed" viewers.
    d) led "distressed" viewers to decompensate (get sicker).

34. One research study on smoking cessation (Jason et al., 1989) found that the best predictor of 12-month abstinence was...
  * a) support group meetings
    b) education
    c) age
    d) job stress

35. The "compressed workweek"...
    a) is another term for a "part-time job"
    b) allows workers total control in choosing where they will work.
    c) is another term for "flexitime."
  * d) typically allows workers to work four days a week.

36. Most university professors select their careers, in part, because of the flexible time constraints. They can often select the hours they work at home versus at the office, with the exception of some key time periods when they must be at school (e.g., for teaching). This schedule is an example of...
  * a) flexitime.
    b) compressed workweeks.
    c) job enlargement.
    d) all of the above.

37. EAP's...
    a) were first developed in the 1980's.
    b) are ineffective.
  * c) can be used in conjunction with wellness programs.
    d) will not help workers with legal problems.

38. Imagine that you are getting bored and disenchanted with your work as fraternity social director. All you do is organize parties for people. In order to increase your job enthusiasm, your fraternity president tells you to organize a new party to celebrate the end of the academic year. This would be an example of...
    a) job enrichment
  * b) job enlargement
    c) meta-analysis
    d) realistic job preview

39. Which of the following is an example of "job enrichment?"
  * a) giving a disenchanted math teacher greater responsibility in shaping the department's new math curriculum.
    b) giving a disenchanted math teacher another section of "introductory mathematics" to teach to a group of freshmen.
    c) offering a disenchanted math teacher a 50% raise in his/her job salary
    d) giving a disenchanted math teacher one extra week of vacation time per year.

40. Zautra and colleagues (1986) found that nurses employed at a psychiatric hospital...
    a) stayed at their jobs as long as there was some stress.
  * b) stayed at stressful jobs as long as the tasks were interesting to them.
    c) avoided interesting work if the job was too stressful.
    d) rated their jobs as more interesting if there was some mild work stress.

41. Shinn and Perkins (in press) reviewed the effects of realistic job preview (RJP) strategies on subsequent job hiring. They found that...
    a. that job applicants did not want to hear about negative aspects of the job.
  * b. RJP had no adverse effects.
    c. new employees were more likely to quit after one month of work if employers shared negative aspects of the job.
    d. both a & c are true.

42. Which of the following statements about "MBO" is true?
    a. The individual employee is solely empowered to make his own decisions.
    b. MBO discourages participative negotiation.
  * c. MBO goals are reviewed to determine whether or not they were too ambitious.
    d. All of the above are true.

43. Porras and colleagues (in press) reviewed almost 50 different studies on organizational development (OD). The authors concluded that...
* a. OD is more beneficial to the organization than to the individual.
  b. OD is more beneficial to the individual than to the organization.
  c. OD is equally beneficial to the organization and to the individual.
  d. OD becomes less effective when more than one method is implemented.

44. According to Golembiewski (1985), the biggest constraint in public sector organizations is ...
* a. procedural rigidity.
  b. MBO
  c. organic systems.
  d. job enlargement.

45. Bennis (1969) advocated for _____ within organizations.
  a. flexitime
  b. quality circles
  c. homework
* d. organic systems

Identification of Terms

1. Beliefs, attitudes, values, and expectations shared by most members of the organization (Answer= Organizational culture).

2. Formal review of an employee's job functioning (Answer= Performance appraisal).

3. Statistical technique for reviewing the literature and evaluating the utility of a practice (Answer= Meta-analysis).

4. Label given to individuals with a chronic sense of time urgency, impatience, competitiveness, and a distaste for idleness (Answer= Type A personality).

5. Term for a work environment which values human dignity and tries to enhance human growth (Answer= Open culture).

6. A term for relapse to drug use (Answer= Recidivism).

7. System in which individual staff and supervisors meet to discuss tasks at hand, to jointly set goals, and to determine how these goals will be met (Answer= Management by objective).

8. Work schedule in which one works Tuesday through Friday, 10 hours per day (Answer= Compressed workweek).

9. Programs designed to prevent health problems before they occur by stressing diet, weight loss, and exercise (Answer= Wellness programs).

10. Adding higher level job responsibilities to an individual's job

repertoire (Answer= Job enrichment).

Food For Thought

I. Imagine that you are the owner of large, multi-million dollar company. Your job is to present an argument in favor of <u>traditional</u> techniques for personnel management. What specific strategies do you support? As an owner, why do you want these techniques?

[Answer notes: Preferred methods include various compensation packages, rules and discipline tactics, and discipline. These methods give you distinct control over the workers.]

II. Now, imagine that you are a community psychologist trying to implement changes in this same company. Using research data, critique the traditional methods of organizational management. What specific techniques would you replace them with?

[Answer notes: Response should reflect the stress, burnout, hostility, and alienation which are often fostered in organizational cultures. Alternatives include QWL programs, MBO, T-groups, etc.]

III. In what ways do organizational and community psychologists share similar goals? In what ways do they differ philosophically and practically?

IV. What are the practical differences between quality circles, T-groups, performance appraisals, and EAP's?

V. Think of someone you know with "burnout." Why did (s)he have burnout? What were the symptoms? Could the burnout have been prevented? If yes, how so?

Key Terms

Brainstorming
Burnout
Compressed workweeks
Constructive feedback
Discharge of employees
Discipline
Employee Assistance Programs (EAP's)
Enabling systems
External pressures to change
Flexitime
Home work
Human Resource Management (HRM)
Internal pressures to change
Job context
Job enlargement
Job enrichment
Management by Objective
Meta-analysis
Networks
Open culture
Organic organizations
Organizational behavior

Organizational culture
Organizational development (OD)
Organizational psychology
Participatory decision making
Performance appraisals
Quality circles
Quality of work life (QWL) programs
Realistic job preview
Recidivism
Reorganization
Repressive culture
Sensitivity groups or T-groups
Social support
Stress
Survey guided feedback
Systems impact
Team building/team development
Termination of employee
Type A/Type B
Umbrella Organizations
Wellness programs
Workaholism
Working to rule
Work schedule adaptations

Recommended Films

Empowering Workers (30 minutes). This program documents businesses which are giving employees more control over management. The benefits of worker empowerment are illustrated, including monetary savings, time savings, reduced absenteeism, and enhanced quality of work. PBS Video, 1320 Braddock Place, Alexandria, VA, 22314-1698. Fax: 703-739-5269.

Locked Out In America: Voices From Ravenswood (30 minutes). A small town in West Virginia is divided when steelworkers at Ravenswood Aluminum Corp. are locked out during negotiations. Illustrates the conflict over labor's right to strike and industry's use of permanent replacements. California Working Group Inc. P.O. Box 10326, Oakland, CA 94610-0326.

Made In America (48 minutes). This program focuses on the story of the assembly line and mass production in the United States. Documents this country's domination of industries such as steelmaking, textile manufacturing, and automobile production using assembly line strategies. PBS Video, 1320 Braddock Place, Alexandria, VA, 22314-1698. Fax: 703-739-5269.

Repowered Employees (60 minutes). This learning program begins by describing the limitations of employee empowerment and, instead, advances an alternative concept called "repowerment." The program uses lectures, role-plays, and a case study technique to demonstrate this approach. PBS Adult Learning Satellite Service, 1320 Braddock Place, Alexandria, VA 22314-1698.

The Workplace (60 minutes). This program explores the importance of the workplace in our society by tracing the evolution of the mills, factories, and office towers of America. PBS Video, 1320 Braddock Place, Alexandria, VA, 22314-1698. Fax: 703-739-5269.

Work Vs. The Family (30 minutes). This program explores companies that are developing ways to help employees balance the demands of work and family. Included are leading businesses which offer on-site daycare and liberal parental leave, flex-time, job sharing, and other nontraditional schedules. PBS Video, 1320 Braddock Place, Alexandria, VA, 22314-1698. Fax: 703-739-5269.

Workforce Diversity (30 minutes). Explores how big businesses are working to promote cultural diversity within the workplace. Illustrates how in-house workshops, assistance networks, and other programs facilitate the greater number of women and other minorities entering business. PBS Video, 1320 Braddock Place, Alexandria, VA, 22314-1698. Fax: 703-739-5269.

CHAPTER 12

THE FUTURE OF COMMUNITY PSYCHOLOGY

Introduction

Philosophical changes within the socio-political arena have had direct implications for the type of social programs funded and disseminated by social service workers. The present chapter introduces the student to the various political and social agenda changes, the effects of these changes, and community psychology's response.

Lectures and Notes

I. Recent Social and Political Agendas Affecting Community Psychology

Throughout the previous three decades there has been a shift in ideological perspective from collectivism to individualism. The change in emphasis from community to personal responsibility regarding the rectification of social problems has been exemplified by the governmental policies of the previous three presidents. The book chapter highlights;
* Ronald Reagan's indirect message of "survival of the fittest" and concomitant reduction in social program spending.
* George Bush's emphasis on volunteerism (e.g., "thousand points of light").
* Bill Clinton's attempt to "re-invent government" and the "new democrats" fiscally responsible yet socially conscious perspective.

Linney (1990), argues that there has been a shift in governmental social program responsibility from the federal to the state levels. The chapter presents both the positive and negative effects of this change including:

Positive Effects
* an unprecedented opportunity for state and local communities to develop innovative approaches to social problems.
* the ability of grass roots citizen groups to develop and successfully implement both prevention and intervention programs with limited resources.
* the increased availability of funding possibilities through private foundations and the need for community psychologists to assist community programs in procuring these funds.

Negative Effects
* the shift in responsibility has led to a fragmentation of social problem agendas. Numerous co-occurring problems (e.g. homelessness and drug addiction) are treated separately, thus large multi-focused programs are unlikely to be developed.
* increased variability in the perspectives concerning which social problems merit attention.
* the sometimes discrepant perspectives of social problems among private sector enterprises, the government, and social scientists which may inhibit progressive social change.

II. General Recommendations About Social Change For The Coming Years

Students are presented with an overview of several issues pertinent to the future direction of community psychology. Specifically, issues concerning social change, prevention, action research, and diversity are discussed.

Social Change

Implementing social change presents a daunting challenge to community activists. However, it is argued that community psychology holds more promise than individual intervention. Students are presented with various methods by which community psychologists can promote social change. These include;
* Information dissemination which may include the utilization of mass media.
* The use of public policy and other legislative action which may enhance the breadth of intervention effects.
* The organization of local interest groups which when called upon can act in unison and may operate on the national level. This is consistent with Heller's (1990) social change solution of <u>regionalization of community building</u>.

IV. <u>Promoting The Values and Goals of Community Psychology Prevention</u>

Primary prevention is one the guiding principles in community psychology. However, while modest gains have been demonstrated towards this end, the goal of complete prevention or elimination has yet to be obtained. Students are presented with the various complications associated with primary prevention research. These include;
* the controversy regarding disorder specific intervention or prevention.
* controversies concerning the most effective preventive strategy including environmental management, the elimination of the causing agent, or strengthening the competence of individuals.
* the best method to address the increasing frequency of comorbid psychiatric disorders and isolating the most effective components of multidimensional prevention programs.

Action Research

Community psychology research entails methodological issues which to some extent differ from the concerns of other areas of psychology. Students are introduced to the methodological concerns associated with action research. Specifically, the non-random selection of volunteers for research projects and small samples studied restrict the generalizability of findings and prohibit community psychologists' to make causal inferences. Students are introduced to the use of meta-analysis which may enhance the ability to discuss causal connections across a wide range of persons, settings, and times. Furthermore, the distinction between outcome and process evaluation is discussed. The ability to evaluate underlying mechanisms by which change occurs can help further the understanding of effective intervention programs and may increase the likelihood of applying such intervention techniques to other affected groups.

Diversity Issues

Community psychologists have suggested that they promote an appreciation of diversity. Previous research studies have documented an increasing trend among published articles concerning ethnic, racial, or religious issues. Recently, a survey of articles published in the <u>American Journal of Community Psychology</u>, between December, 1992 to October, 1993, found that 38% of the articles pertained to groups other than White Americans (Duffy & Wong, 1995). Students are presented with the idea that as a field community psychology should continue to promote an appreciation for diversity and develop intervention and preventive programs that are sensitive to the particular needs and issues of diverse cultures.

Multiple Choice

1. The ideological perspective that holds people are responsible for their own actions is known as _____.
    a. collectivism   * c. individualism
    b. independency   d. isolationism

2. The ideological perspective that holds many people share the responsibility for addressing social problems is known as _____.
  * a. collectivism   c. individualism
    b. socialism   d. communism

3. The ideological shift from _____ to _____ has resulted in a concurrent reordering of governmental responsibility towards social problems.
    a. individualism; collectivism   b. socialism; capitalism
  * c. collectivism; individualism   d. personal; group

4. Throughout the past decade there has been a shift in governmental responsibility from the _____ level to _____ level concerning social problems.
    a. community; state   c. state; federal
  * b. federal; state   d. federal; community

5. Economic pressures have inhibited the government from continuing the strong and consistent support for preventive services.
    a. True   * b. False

6. The shifting in governmental responsibility for social problems can be perceived as primarily a _____ occurrence.
    a. negative   c. positive
  * b. both a and c   d. none of the above

7. The effect(s) of the shifting of governmental responsibility has been to _____.
    a. create the opportunity for more flexible and innovative social programs.
    b. increased the need for grant consultants
    c. fragmented available funding and preventive approaches
    d. both a and b
  * e. all of the above

8. Studies have demonstrated that many individuals in need of social service assistance suffer from a _____ problem(s).
    a. singular   * c. multiple set of
    b. specific   d. none of the above

9. Fragmentation of governmental funding has resulted in the development of _____ programs.
	a. multi-focused c. comprehensive
 * b. narrowly focused d. both a and c

10. The _____ of funding services is an important goal for the future in the field of community psychology.
	a. fragmentation c. partitioning
	b. overlapping * d. coordination

11. Current difficulties associated with the provision of social services include(s) _____.
	a. differing perspectives of what constitutes a social problem
	b. overlapping service provision
	c. the fragmentation of service programs
	d. both a and c
 * e. all of the above

12. The Anti-Smoking campaign provides a good example of a unified social problem agenda and a successful preventive strategy.
	a. True * b. False

13. According to the text's authors, community intervention holds _____ promise than individual intervention for various social problems.
 * a. more   c. equitable
	b. less d. none of the above

14. When implementing intervention programs within the community, psychologists should consider
	a. the governmental responsibility
 * b. community beliefs and values
	c. the effect of service fragmentation
	d. both a and b
	e. all of the above

15. Ways in which community psychologists can accelerate change include(s) _____.
	a. replicating and refining previously implemented programs.
	b. disseminate information regarding various interventions through journals and conferences.
	c. the utilization of mass media
	d. both a and b
 * e. all of the above

16. The promotion of large-scale community change can be facilitated through the use of _____.
	a. public policy c. mass media
	b. legislative action * d. all of the above
	e. both a and b

17. The tendency of community psychologists to "think _____" has restricted the use of many possibilities facilitating community change.
* a. small
c. globally
b. large
d. generally

18. Although developed to address a wide range of social problems, comprehensive federal social programs have been criticized for
a. ignoring local values or concerns
b. providing overlapping services
c. ignoring private enterprise agendas
d. both a and c
* e. both a and b

19. _____ refers to the use of loose-knit, large scale confederations of local groups which when coordinated can influence policy at the national level.
a. social unionization
b. regional coordination
* c. regionalization of community building
d. grass-root lobbying

20. According to Heller (1990), _____ is an example of a social solution which provides sensitivity to local concerns yet affords more power than local communities.
* a. Mothers Against Drunk Driving
b. The State Senate
c. Boards of Education
d. Alcoholics Anonymous

21. A social change solution offered by Heller (1990), which is based upon the use of coalition building is known as _____.
a. social unionization
* b. regionalization of community building
c. lobbying
d. political activism

22. Dr. Jane has developed a program for which the goal is to decrease the initial occurrence of alcohol use. Her program would be considered a___ _____ prevention technique.
a. secondary
* c. primary
b. tertiary
d. clinical

23. _____ programs refer to activities that can be undertaken with a healthy population to maintain or enhance their physical or emotional health.
a. Secondary prevention
c. Tertiary prevention
b. Social prevention
* d. Primary prevention

24. The consensus among community psychologists concerning the most effective primary preventive strategy is the use of_____.
a. environmental modification
b. enhancing individual competence
c. elimination of the cause of the problem
d. both a and c
* e. none of the above

25. The use of primary prevention strategies has resulted in the elimination of several major disorders and social problems.
   a. True   * b. False

26. Preventive strategies employed by community psychologists include:
   a. modifying the environment
   b. eliminating the agent or cause of the problem
   c. enhancing the skills of the affected individual
   d. both a and c
   * e. all of the above

27. _____ refers to the instances in which individuals present with more than one mental disorder.
   a. Multiple personality disorder
   * b. Comorbidity
   c. Concurrent diagnoses
   d. none of the above

28. A controversy concerning the various preventive and intervention approaches for those individuals presenting with more than one mental disorder include(s):
   a. how to isolate the effective elements of a particular strategy
   b. whether primary prevention should be disorder specific
   c. discerning what intervention components are most useful with what disorders
   d. both b and c
   * e. all of the above

29. The use of _____ samples allows for better causal inferences in both field and laboratory experiments.
   * a. random   c. community
   b. volunteer   d. "real-life"

30. A sample in which every member of a particular population has an equal chance of being selected is known as a _____ sample.
   a. volunteer   c. unbiased
   b. research   * d. random

31. Dr. John would like to examine the effects of commuting stress on workers who travel into the city. He decides to walk to the limousine company and interview those who are chauffeured to work. The results indicate that commuting produces very little stress for all workers going to the city. This inference is most likely invalid because he _____.
   a. based the study on a random sample of workers
   * b. failed to randomly select workers
   c. used the wrong measure for stress
   d. this would be an accurate conclusion

32. Community psychologists are most likely to be involved in _____ research, which is designed to resolve social problems.
   a. community
   b. laboratory
   * c. action
   d. field

33. The challenges facing community psychologists regarding the particular research they conduct include
   a. restricted causal inferences
   b. the use of non-random samples
   c. the development of new statistical procedures to improve the generalizability of their findings
   d. both a and c
   * e. all of the above

34. _____ refers to a statistical procedure which allows psychologists to examine a particular concept or intervention across varying settings, times, and persons.
   a. Experimentation
   b. Correlation
   * c. Meta-analysis
   d. Process-analysis

35. Difficulties associated with action research include(s) _____.
   a. non-randomization
   b. diverse methodologies
   c. small samples
   * d. all of the above
   e. both a and c

36. _____ analysis refers to the study of the underlying mechanisms by which change occurs.
   * a. Process
   b. Experimental
   c. Meta
   d. Factor

37. According to the text, a majority of the research concerning community intervention programs can be classified as _____ research.
   a. process
   * b. outcome
   c. experimental
   d. tertiary

38. A recent study conducted by the text author's indicates community psychology has demonstrated a(n) _____ trend concerning issues relating to ethnic diversity.
   a. stable
   c. decreasing
   * d. increasing
   d. moderate

39. Results of a recent survey of the _American Journal of Community Psychology_ indicated that approximately, _____ percent of the articles pertained to groups other than White Americans.
   a. 10
   b. 90
   * c. 38
   d. 76

40. The promotion of the "appreciation of ethnic diversity" by community psychologists has been strongly demonstrated in both the type of programs implemented and research articles published.
   a. True
   * b. False

Identification of Terms

1. The ideological perspective in which people are ultimately responsible for their own actions. [Answer= individualism]

2. The ideological perspective in which the community shares the responsibility for addressing social problems. [Answer= collectivism]

3. One of the guiding principles of community psychology which refers to the attempts to prevent a problem prior to its occurrence. [Answer= primary prevention]

4. A social change solution which incorporates local community concerns and provides more power to individuals to influence public policy. [Answer= regionalization of community building]

5. A statistical analysis which emphasizes the robustness of a particular causal connection across a wide range of persons, settings, and times. [Answer= meta-analysis]

6. Research which is designed to highlight and resolve social problems. [Answer= action research]

7. A type of sample used in research in which every member of a particular population has an equal chance of being selected. [Answer=random sample]

8. A method in which the underlying mechanisms responsible for producing change are the focus of study. [Answer= process analysis]

9. A community psychology program developed to increase citizen activity in their localities through building of self-study research and evaluation skills. [Answer= Social Reconnaissance]

10. The term used to describe the phenomena in which individuals manifest more than one disorder concurrently. [Answer= comorbidity of psychiatric disorders]

Food for Thought

I. Many have argued that a particular culture's conceptualization and treatment of "social ills" is strongly related to the political and social agenda set for that time period. Discuss how this statement may apply to community psychology over the past two decades. (Answer Notes= students may discuss the previous presidents and their associated policies. Discussion may also include the shift from federal to state levels)

II. The shift in governmental responsibility concerning social program funding has effected intervention programs in numerous ways. Discuss what this shift was and both the positive and negative effects associated with this change. (Answer Notes= students should describe the federal to state shift in responsibility and positive effects such as the increased use of grass root organizations and negative effects such as fragmentation of agendas)

III. Community psychology has been presented with the challenge of developing and implementing new and innovative programs to address both the current and future needs of society. As a community psychologist describe the specific issue that may concern you and pose a challenge to your profession. (Answer Notes= students should discuss issues concerning social change, prevention, action research, and diversity)

IV. As a community psychologist you have just been hired to develop a prevention and social change program focusing on adolescent drug and alcohol abuse. Describe some of the issues you may have to address and outline the various methods you would use to implement your program. (Answer Notes= students may include among others the use of mass media, the possible problems of comorbidity, and the inclusion or use of public policy)

Key Terms

Action research
Collectivism
Individualism
Meta-analysis
Primary prevention
Process analysis
Random sample
Regionalization of community building
Social Reconnaissance

Recommended Films

The Issue Is Race (120 minutes). This program combines a panel discussion and town hall format with documentary video segments to discuss racial problems and racial relations over the past 25 years. Films for the Humanities & Sciences , P.O. Box 2053, Princeton, NJ, 08543-2053.

Mirrors of the Heart: Race and Identity (60 minutes). Explores race and ethnicity as indicators of an individual's self image and social standing. People of neighboring Haiti and the Dominican Republic show contrasting attitudes towards their African roots. Part 4 of the Latin America series. Corporation for Public Broadcasting: The Annenberg/CPB Project, 901 E Street, NW, Washington D.C., 20004-2037.

The Challenge of Livable Communities: Revitalizing Urban Environments Through Historic Preservation: (Two 60 minute programs). This two-part series includes a provocative "urban roundtable" on societal issues that asks whether cities are, in fact, obsolete. PBS Adult Learning Satellite Service. PBS 1320 Braddock Place, Alexandria, VA 22314-1698.

Introduction to Culture and Diversity (60 minutes). Defining the terms culture, macroculture, and microculture, this discussion considers the many cultures and religious groups in the United States. Students discuss the dangers of viewing other cultures from an ethocentric point of view.

Is Cultural Diversity a Good Idea? (30 minutes). This films highlights discussions concerning the desirability of cultural diversity. Issues concerning the education of minorities and women for industry jobs as discussed. Insight Media Inc., 2162 Broadway, New York, New York, 10024.